"They Watch Me as They Watch This"

"They Watch Me as They Watch This"

Gertrude Stein's Metadrama

Jane Palatini Bowers

upp

UNIVERSITY OF PENNSYLVANIA PRESS   Philadelphia

Grateful acknowledgment is extended to the Estate of Gertrude Stein for permission to quote from previously published letters of Gertrude Stein to Carl Van Vechten and from the texts of *Geography and Plays* and *How to Write*.

Grateful acknowledgment is extended to the Collection of American Literature, Beinecke Rare Book and Manuscript Library, Yale University, for permission to quote from unpublished letters and manuscripts of Gertrude Stein and from a typescript of a tape-recorded interview of Gertrude Stein by William Lundell for NBC.

Grateful acknowledgment is extended to Louis R. Barbato, Associate Professor of English, Cleveland State University, for permission to quote from "Gertrude Stein's Operas," an unpublished paper.

Grateful acknowledgment is also made to the following:

Random House, Inc., for permission to quote from *Lectures in America*, *The Autobiography of Alice B. Toklas*, *Everybody's Autobiography*, *The Geographical History of America*, and *Last Operas and Plays*, by Gertrude Stein.

Yale University Press, for permission to quote from *Bee Time Vine*, by Gertrude Stein.

Kathleen Barry and New York University Press, for permission to quote from *Susan B. Anthony: A Biography of a Singular Feminist*, by Kathleen Barry. Copyright © 1988 by Kathleen Barry.

Liveright Publishing Corp., for permission to quote from *Fernhurst, Q.E.D., and Other Early Writings*, by Gertrude Stein. Copyright © 1971 by Daniel C. Joseph, Administrator of the Estate of Gertrude Stein.

Edward Burns, for permission to quote from *Staying on Alone: Letters of Alice B. Toklas*. Published by Liveright Publishing Corp., 1973.

Twayne Publishers, a division of G. K. Hall & Co., for permission to adapt material originally published as "The Writer in the Theater: Gertrude Stein's *Four Saints in Three Acts*," by Jane Bowers, in *Critical Essays on Gertrude Stein*, Michael Hoffman, ed. Copyright © 1986 by Twayne Publishers.

Library of Congress Cataloging-in-Publication Data

Bowers, Jane Palatini.
  "They watch me as they watch this": Gertrude Stein's metadrama / Jane Palatini Bowers.
      p.   cm.
  Includes bibliographical references and index.
  ISBN 0-8122-3057-4
  1. Stein, Gertrude, 1874–1946—Dramatic works. 2. Experimental drama—History and criticism. I. Title.
PS3537.T323Z558   1991   91-9165
812'.52—dc20   CIP

For my father
OSWALD C. PALATINI
1903–1990

Contents

Acknowledgments

In 1975 in a graduate seminar at Berkeley on Anglo-American modernism, Frederick Crews assigned an article by David Antin, "Some Questions about Modernism," in which Antin stated that "Gertrude Stein was the only truly modernist writer we [America] had." My book on Stein's plays really began when I read that startling pronouncement. Antin's revision of the modernist canon, placing Stein at the center rather than the periphery, a revision hotly debated among the graduate students in Professor Crews's seminar, helped me to see a different literary history from the one I had previously studied and gave me a sense of mission which has sustained me through years of work with Stein's texts.

While still a graduate student at Berkeley, I was fortunate to be able to work with Richard Bridgman and Jayne Walker. I not only profited by their careful reading of my dissertation, from which this book has evolved, but I was also inspired by the standard of scholarly excellence they set in their own books on Stein. Later I had the pleasure of meeting and working with another fine Stein scholar, Michael Hoffman, without whose advice and encouragement I might never have begun the task of revising my dissertation. Catharine Stimpson read my entire manuscript two times, and her meticulous and thoughtful criticism of it was invaluable in guiding me as I revised. Ulla Dydo and Carol Stanger read portions of the manuscript and made a number of helpful suggestions. I would especially like to thank Marjorie Perloff. Her brilliant book, *The Poetics of Indeterminacy*, has shaped my thinking about Stein and about modernist and postmodernist writers. Beyond my intellectual debt to her, I am also indebted to her personally for her generous response to my work.

I have been delighted with the editors at the University of Pennsylvania Press: thanks to Jerry Singerman for his wise management of my manuscript and his unfailing good humor; and to Ruth Veleta, the manuscript editor, and David Prout, the copyeditor, for their skill. Being so good at their jobs, they have made mine much easier.

For all these colleagues, teachers, and friends who have nourished my mind and improved my writing, I am truly grateful. But there are others to whom I am more grateful still whose presence in my life made the thinking and writing possible.

I am extremely thankful for my association with Robert Herman. We have collaborated productively for three years during which we did not "cease from Mental Fight." I would like to thank Harry Bowers, a one-man foundation, for making it possible for me to take a year off from teaching to begin work on this book. Finally, I want to thank my children, John and Chloë. John, who was born while I was still an undergraduate, has been my partner from the beginning in this business of launching an academic career, and although I seem to be the one reaping the most tangible rewards, I hope that he too has benefited as he has enriched me. I am grateful for Chloë's loving companionship during the writing of this book. She is a splendid daughter and an extraordinary friend.

Introduction

In this book I discuss Gertrude Stein's writing in a single genre: drama. Stein's plays have often been the subject of individual chapters (or parts of chapters) in critical works assessing her entire career or specific periods of it.[1] Some of these works divide Stein's plays into two types: dialogues and landscapes. Others ignore the early dialogue plays and focus on the later landscapes, in particular *Four Saints in Three Acts*. While *Four Saints* is an undeniably important play in the Stein canon, it has less in common with other so-called landscape plays than most Stein critics would have us believe. Since other plays are seldom given much attention, the variety within the designation "landscape plays" is often overlooked. The discussion of Stein's plays, and of her work in other genres, has been inadequate when little attention has been paid to the variety of the texts in that genre and when genre has served, as it often has, as a more or less arbitrary way of classifying Stein's writing. It is no wonder then that in recent years many Stein scholars have turned away from genre. "Genre won't do," writes Bruce Kellner in his introduction to *A Gertrude Stein Companion*,[2] and Marianne DeKoven argues that "the division of her [Stein's] work into chronological styles is much more meaningful than the division into works or genres."[3] I believe, however, that a generic approach to Stein's work can yield particularly rich insights into her writing itself and into the genres she used.

Stein once advised an aspiring writer to "think of the writing in terms of discovery."[4] That advice was based on her own practice since, for Stein, writing was discovery. When the process of discovery was undertaken in a preexisting literary genre, Stein was exploring territory that had already been carefully mapped. The conventions of the genre mark the way. Nonetheless, a writer who is a discoverer must strike out on her own, away from the well-worn paths of the mapmakers. This Stein did. Her plays are like nothing that ever came before them, and they are exciting in their newness, in the ways in which they depart from convention, and even from other unconventional drama. Yet, for all their strangeness, they are still plays, for Stein did not abandon the conventions of the genre entirely; rather, she questioned them and the limits they imposed on the free play of language and creation. The interplay between her texts and the conventions of the genre leads Stein to make discoveries about the genre, and these discoveries give her plays their value as theater texts. If we failed to consider them generically, we might miss these discoveries, and that would be a great loss not only to Stein scholarship but also to theater scholarship.

There is one book-length work on Stein's writing for the theater: Betsy Alayne Ryan's *Gertrude Stein's Theatre of the Absolute*. Ryan's focus on genre is welcome, but I disagree with her thesis that Stein's "plays, as distinguished from the novels and portraits, . . . are physical expressions whose realization lay not on the printed page, but in live performance. For full impact, they have to be seen. . . . In the theatre the plays exist as simple, concrete phenomena."[5] According to Ryan: "The theatre that she [Stein] enjoyed and respected was concrete, dynamic, and absolutely present, capturing in essence what traditional theatre was content to describe linearly. Her own plays would be based strictly upon this conception, and would embody it."[6] This idea that Stein's plays are pure theater, in harmony with the physicality and immediacy of performance, is a common misperception about these texts. The misperception arises because of Stein's own comments about the visual excitement and immediacy of the theater and because of her own account of having been inspired to write plays by dance performances and bullfights.[7] The staging of Stein's plays and their frequent musical accompaniment have only reinforced this misperception. However, Stein's plays are not "physical expressions"; they do not emphasize or even facilitate the physical realization of the play on a stage. In fact, Stein's plays oppose the physicality of performance. Stein's is a theater of language: her plays are adamantly and self-consciously "literary," as I will show through close readings of her texts.

I present these readings chronologically because Stein's process of discovery unfolds through time, new discoveries evolving from old. The first chapter deals with the earliest plays, which I have called "conversation" plays, written between 1915 and 1919. I have not called them dialogues, as is often done. Even though they present the alternating addresses and responses of speaking partners, this conversation differs profoundly from conventional dramatic dialogue. The second and longest chapter covers plays written between 1920 and 1933—the bulk of Stein's writing for the theater. Stein called these plays "landscapes"; I call them "lang-scapes." I have adapted her term to more closely reflect the "subject" of these plays, which is not the "land" around her country home in Bilignin, as Stein sometimes claimed, but rather language in the theater. The lang-scape plays are of two types: those from 1920 to 1923, which are concerned with the spatiality of theater art and the ways in which the written text and performance text function in performance space, and those from 1927 to 1933, which are concerned with the temporality of theater art and the ways in which the text functions in performance time. In chapter 3 I discuss two texts which are not plays but which are about plays—the lecture "Plays" and the book *The Geographical History of America*—and two plays—*Not and Now* and *Listen to Me*, written between 1934 and 1936. In chapter 4 I consider two anomalous plays: *Doctor Faustus Lights the Lights* and *The Mother of Us All*, written in 1938 and 1945, respectively. Like Marianne DeKoven, I believe that toward the end of her life Stein turned to "specifically female material, and perhaps feminist intention."[8] *Doctor Faustus* and *The Mother of Us All* certainly call for the feminist reading I give them.

It is possible, of course, to interpret Stein's experimentation and her self-reflexivity as feminist. DeKoven does, in fact, argue that Stein's experiments with linguistic structures are antipatriarchal inasmuch as they disrupt "the privileged language of patriarchy."[9] Harriet Chessman, another feminist critic of Stein, characterizes the self-reflexiveness of Stein's work as a "dialogue between the writer and words" and as a "paradigm of 'creation' as a shared and ongoing creative process, in which the creative act mingles inextricably with the created writing."[10] Following a logic similar to DeKoven's, Chessman interprets Stein's "poetics of dialogue," which includes the metadiscursive "dialogue between the writer and words," as "an alternative to the possibility of patriarchal authoritarianism implicit in monologue."[11] In identifying Stein's experimentation and metadiscursiveness as antipatriarchal, both writers make a case for an implicit feminism in Stein's work. Yet both writers acknowledge that Stein's feminism is debatable precisely because it is implicit. As Chessman writes, "In calling Stein's project 'feminist,' I am entering a lively and ongoing debate about whether Stein *is* feminist. . . . Stein does not help us out directly."[12] Chessman cautions that "to move too quickly or easily from interpretations of her identity to judgments about the 'feminist' or 'unfeminist' nature of her writing seems dangerous." Nonetheless, Chessman joins her voice to DeKoven's and to the "growing consensus . . . among many critics of Stein that her writing, particularly after about 1910, reveals a feminist concern with gender hierarchy, a system of domination allied with the dominance of certain narrative and linguistic forms over others."[13]

Stein's writing for the theater, considered from a generic perspective, can show us just how concerned Stein was to oppose, subvert, and disrupt the dominant, conventional forms of drama. But I hesitate to identify this concern as "feminist," unless I were to go as far as DeKoven does and to declare that "opposition to patriarchal modes seems . . . the ultimate *raison d'être* for all experimental writing."[14] However, to equate feminism and experimentalism, to enlist feminism under the experimentalist banner, as DeKoven seems to do, is to undermine the political agenda of feminism and of those writers (and critics) who do make a claim, as Stein does not, for their "writing as addressing or redressing women's position (or repression) within culture" and who do acknowledge, as Stein does not, the "biological or gender distinction as a real or important one."[15] Moreover, since all experimental writers disrupt the conventions of discourse, as Stein does, and since metadiscursiveness often plays a part in this disruption, as it does in Stein's work, it seems more accurate to describe Stein's project as experimentalist (or modernist) than as feminist. I approach Stein's work, as I believe Stein approached it, with an interest in her process of creation itself and in her discovery, through experimentation, of new ways of making language and literature. This approach has led me to see the plays written between 1915 and 1936 not as implicitly feminist texts but as self-reflexive plays that question the way language functions in the theater and that are concerned with the interaction between textuality and performance.

Because these plays are about language in the theater, they are metadramas. They are not metadramas in the narrowest sense of the term, as defined by Lionel Abel in *Metatheatre*, that is, "theatre pieces about life seen as already theatricalized," plays marked by a deliberate theatricality and by the use of explicit devices, such as the play within the play, to call the audience's attention to the theatricality of the play and ultimately to the artifice of life.[16] Rather, Stein's plays are metadramas in a broader sense as defined by Susan Wittig in her essay "Toward a Semiotic Theory of Drama," by Patrice Pavis in *Languages of the Stage*, by James Calderwood in his series of books on Shakespearean metadrama, and by Richard Hornby in *Drama, Metadrama, and Perception*. Metadrama is more broadly defined by these writers as drama that is self-referential and self-reflexive. Quite simply, metadrama is, as Hornby writes, "drama about drama."[17] A metadramatic text will, according to Pavis, "inscribe" its own reading (i.e., interpretation) "within the text to be read" through a "descriptive and interpretive metalanguage" which can take several forms, of which an image of the work within the work itself (play within a play) is but one.[18] Metadrama will call attention to its own construction. Not only will the play be a discourse about its ostensible subject, it will also be a discourse about "dramatic art itself—its materials, its media of language and theater, its generic forms and conventions, its relationship to truth and the social order."[19]

Wittig goes so far as to claim that "*all* artistic drama is metatheatre, drama cast in a self-conscious medium" and that all aesthetic discourse (as distinguished from popular discourse) is metadiscursive—"conscious of itself as a made thing."[20] It is true, as Calderwood notes, that "in a sense each poem contains its own poetics,"[21] a truth that Wittig emphasizes in her essay. But I would like to make the case for Stein's plays (as Calderwood does for Shakespeare's) that they are metadramatic in a special sense. Metadiscursiveness is not simply an underlying characteristic of Stein's plays that they share with all drama; rather, discourse about the role of language in the theater is Stein's consistent preoccupation in her plays.

It is this metadiscursiveness more than any other characteristic of her work, I believe, which has made Stein an important influence on post-modern dramatists, mixed-media artists, and performance poets, an influence I discuss in my concluding chapter. Pavis writes that in post-modernist texts "the question is the only message and the text is constituted by dint of reflection on its possibility."[22] This could serve just as well as a description of Stein's play texts: they constantly pose questions about and reflect on the possibility of writing for the theater. David Antin has argued persuasively that this questioning is the quintessential quality of modern art as well. He calls modern art an art of "exemplary presentation." According to Antin, "Modernism is definable in terms of a single fundamental axiom: that it is necessary to begin from a radical act of definition or redefinition of the domain of the elements and the operations of the art or of art itself."[23] Most of Stein's writing exhibits this quality of "exemplary presentation," with definition and redefinition taking place in the domain of linguistic structures. When she was writing in a particular genre, the domain was extended to include generic structures.

Stein not only wrote about language in the theater, but also wrote plays in which she foregrounded language, moving to the background the other elements of the performance: scenic space, actor, and action. In the conversation plays, speech is foregrounded; in the lang-scape plays, the foreground is the text, the words written to be read and spoken. We are always conscious of the existence of that text as a part of the performance. The writer and her writing are brought into the theater through the text.

In attempting to foreground the text, Stein encountered the sine qua non of the theater event: a text, the structure created by the writer, must become part of an action, the performance by the actors. Word and act must meet in the theater, and their meeting is a central preoccupation of anyone writing for or about the theater. Some see this duality of the theater event as built into the text (dramatic language, as Pierre Larthomas writes, is "a compromise between two languages, the written and the spoken");[24] others see in the theater two kinds of text: the written text (a script) and the performance text (the realization of that script on the stage). Whether one characterizes the relationship between written text and performance as one of "mutual and shifting constraints between two kinds of text, neither of which is prior and neither of which is precisely 'immanent' within the other,"[25] or as "a synthesis of the opposition between the mental representation evoked by the word and the pragmatic reality projected on the stage,"[26] or as a "transformation" and "iconization (*mise en vue*) of the word,"[27] or as a "dialectical tension between the dramatic text and the actor,"[28] the interrelatedness of word and act is, as Jindřich Honzl writes, an "enduring law of theatrical creativity and perception."[29]

What was the effect of this "law" on the language of Gertrude Stein, a poet whose only acquaintance with the theater came as a member of the audience, when she attempted to foreground language against the other elements of theater art? However theorists characterize the relationship between word and act, they agree that language is diminished in some way by its contact with action.

Jiří Veltruský writes:

In theater, the sign created by the actor tends, because of its overwhelming reality, to monopolize the attention of the audience at the expense of the immaterial meanings conveyed by the linguistic sign; it tends to divert attention from the text to the voice performance, from speeches to physical actions and even to the physical appearance of the stage figure.[30]

Here is André Helbo on the same subject:

The text effectively loses its value as a descriptive-narrative instrument preceded by a situation and is transformed into relays of the miming function which confers scenic existence to the interlocutors.[31]

Or Keir Elam:

Language loses all its exclusive privileges and has instead to share them with the co-operating or rival *langues* such as gesture.

That is not to say, Elam continues, that language

suffers any actual or absolute loss of *power*. . . . It is rather to emphasise that it is no longer indispensable as a means of initiating articulated semiosis, and must accede to a general semiotic process to which it is subordinate.[32]

Patrice Pavis describes the effect of action on language this way:

The text is revealed in all its fragility, constantly menaced . . . by gestuality which might at any time interrupt its emission, and which always guides the spectator in the rhythm of his reception.[33]

And James Calderwood writes:

The poet has a great advantage over the dramatist, for whereas the poet may carefully supervise the preservation of his words in print, . . . in the dramatist's medium of the stage his words dissolve even as they are formed—dissolve and fall back into the great public reservoir of language where he originally found them and where they resume their referential status as signs.[34]

Overwhelmed, transformed, subordinated, menaced, and dissolved—the various fates of language in the theater. In her plays Stein sought to rescue language from these and similar fates.

Chapter 1

The Conversation Plays: 1915 to 1919

In 1935 Gertrude Stein toured the United States giving a series of lectures in which she explained her work in various genres and her ideas about painting, poetry, and grammar, among other things. In one of these lectures, "Plays," she announced the genesis of the more than eighty plays she was eventually to write. She declared, "And so one day all of a sudden I began to write Plays."[1] Her clear generic demarcation of plays and nonplays does not quite accord with what we can see when we read those very first plays.

In fact, *White Wines, A Curtain Raiser,* and *What Happened,* the three plays Stein wrote in 1913, are textually similar to *Tender Buttons,* the collection of verbal still lifes she had written between 1910 and 1912.[2] In these plays, as in her still lifes, Stein favors definition as the chief rhetorical mode and naming as the chief linguistic activity. Definition, a static mode that immobilizes the subject, would seem better suited to still life than to drama, an art form whose essence is action.[3]

Stein's only apparent accommodation to the dramatic genre in these first plays is her division of the texts into "acts" and into a main text which will eventually be spoken and a side text of character ascriptions and stage directions. Accordingly, *What Happened* has five acts. Within each act, the main text is divided into sections preceded by parenthetical numbers. These are not scene numbers; rather they seem to specify the number of speakers to whom the text is to be assigned ("One," "Five," "Three," "The Same Three").[4] In *White Wines,* a three-act play, Stein makes character ascriptions more specific ("witnesses," "more witnesses," "5 women") and adds some tentative stage directions ("all together," "house to house").[5] These formal dramatic conventions seem to be superimposed on texts that exhibit no other sign of having been dramatically conceived.

Moreover, the supposed sudden beginning of her playwriting

which Stein recalled as having happened on a day in 1913 was only a fitful start. After the three short plays of 1913, Stein did not write another play until 1915. In the meantime she was continuing her work in another genre, the literary portrait, and developing what Wendy Steiner has called a "hybrid form"—the dialogue portrait, a kind of "exercise" for playwriting.[6]

Stein herself commented on the connection between her portraits and the plays which began to emerge from them:

> I had before I began writing plays written many portraits. I had been enormously interested all my life in finding out what made each one that one and so I had written a great many portraits.
>
> I came to think that since each one is that one and that there are a number of them each one being that one, the only way to express this thing each one being that one and there being a number of them knowing each other was in a play. And so I began to write these plays.[7]

The manuscript of a group portrait called "Jenny, Helen, Hannah, Paul and Peter," which Stein began writing in 1912, shows the process by which Stein came to think that the way to express "each one" and "them knowing each other" was in a play. On the flyleaf of the first of five composition notebooks she filled with this portrait, Stein lists the subjects of the portrait: "Jenny, Helen, Hannah, Paul and Peter / Lana, Miriam, Adele, Ben & Joe." As she begins to write she simply names the subject(s) within the portrait:

> All five of them were living. All five of them had been living.
>
> Jenny and Helen had been living. Jenny was the older. Helen was the younger. Jenny was much older. She was older and had been living. She was older, she went on being living. She was older, she went on being living. Helen was younger.[8]

Stein filled the entire first notebook with the portrait of Jenny and Helen, who are referred to after the first few pages by the ambiguous "she" which has the effect of merging the identities of the two.

In the second notebook, Stein begins to write of Jenny and Helen as "they" or as "each one of the two of them," expressing both their relatedness and their separateness. Halfway through this notebook and across the top of a clean page, Stein tries a new way of indicating the relationship between the "ones" in her portrait: "Miriam's attitude toward Lana (living and feeling) anger and distrust and anyone and fear and understanding."[9] Further headings appear, describing the "attitude" of one person toward another, the feelings Stein would try to convey in her portrait. Some headings simply name the ones to be written about. Some read like Stein's instructions to herself: "Go on to other things they do just, or not just because," or "Go on with the relationship between Lana and Miriam."[10] In the third notebook, names sometimes give way to an indefinite notation: "Each one in relation to anybody." Individuals join, separate, and re-combine in different configurations: "More M. & Adele, then Adele. Joe. Ben." In the third notebook Stein also begins to use a sort of shorthand to indicate the subjects of the portrait. Above the sections of text appear initials, "B. A. M. J."—for Ben, Adele, Miriam, and Joe; then later, "(Adele) B. A. M. J."; and still later "(B. A.) M. J." These notations look like some abstract geometry of relationship, as though Stein were trying to plot the very movement of relationship rather than the feelings and attitudes she had earlier recorded. Also in the third notebook Stein begins to put names in parentheses, much as she did the "stage directions" and vocal ascriptions of the 1913 plays, *White Wines* and *What Happened*. Headings that call for portraits— "(Ben & Adele) (Their life) (their character)"—alternate with head-ings that seem like directions for a choreography of relationships— "(Ben, then Adele to all, Ben to all)."[11]

By the time she reached the fifth and last notebook, Stein had apparently realized the drama inherent in the shifting relationships she had been cataloguing. Headings read, "Drama everyone M.," and "Drama L & M again and M everyone." "Make it dramatic. Not char-acters, relations," she instructs herself.[12] The manuscript of "Jenny, Helen, Hannah, Peter and Paul" literally records the fact that Stein's interest in group portraits gave rise to her interest in drama.

In writing her way from her portraits of relationships like "Jenny, Helen, Hannah, Peter and Paul" to the conversation plays of 1915 to 1919, Stein made a number of adjustments in her style. She began to reproduce speech within the portraits. Then she began to break up the text to emphasize the give-and-take of dialogue; she also began to limit herself to dialogue as a mode of expression.[13] Finally, she eliminated herself as the "portraitist-perceiver" within the text. Steiner points to this last but most important difference between di-alogue portraits and conversation plays. She also suggests that Stein took on a new role to replace the old, that of a speaker in the dia-logue. Undeniably, Stein's voice is often heard in these plays, but one could hardly describe them as dialogic exchanges between one char-acter, Gertrude Stein, and other characters. Stein functions more like a court reporter than a fellow actor; the plays seem like transcriptions of what she hears. As Richard Bridgman has observed, to listen to these plays is like listening to a tape recording made over the course of several hours in a room of an unidentified and unfamiliar house-hold.[14] The identity of the person who supplied and activated the machine is irrelevant, though we may indeed be hearing her voice among the others. Since none of the voices is identified for us, we cannot tell for certain whose voices we are hearing. We may guess that the voices belong to particular people from various clues they drop in the course of the recording, but such deductions are never facilitated or validated by the text, and again, they are irrelevant. Of course, Stein's posture as scribe or recording secretary is a pretense. Stein's plays, like all plays, like all poetry in fact, are not natural but fictive utterances.[15] These seeming conversations are artifacts created by Gertrude Stein. This pretense of naturalness is at the heart of dramatic mimesis, and Stein's plays at once engage in and expose it.

Stein said that her "idea" in writing plays was "to express . . . each one being that one and there being a number of them knowing each other . . . without telling what happened, in short to make a play the essence of what happened."[16] We might expect a play intended to be the "essence of what happened" to be a play full of action, of "happenings." This expectation is further reinforced by Stein's claim that she was inspired to write plays by her attendance at bullfights and dance performances. These visual, action-packed events reminded her that there is "something going on at a theater."[17]

This "something going on" is not to be confused with a story. Stein flatly declared that she did not want her plays to tell stories. In a sense, of course, no play "tells" a story. Rather, the language of the play is the story; as it is spoken, the dialogue creates the world of the play and the state of affairs in that world, or as Stein put it, the dialogue is "what made what happened be what it was."[18] That is why drama has been considered the most mimetic mode—because in it language comes as close as it ever can in literature to being a present action with immediate consequences, rather than a representation, after the fact, of nonlinguistic actions, states, and objects.

But as Stein's conversation plays demonstrate, the mimetic theory of drama rests on a fallacy. In fact, the "story" precedes and shapes the dialogue of even, and perhaps especially, the most natural-seeming, the most mimetic plays. Dramatic dialogue is not primary and constitutive, but secondary and derivative, not a natural phenomenon but an artificial one. In order, then, for a play text to be the essence of what happened, which is what Stein hoped her plays would be, "what happened" must be a linguistic event, a speech act, because, with respect to other kinds of events and acts, language can only be a report or a response, but not the thing itself. Stein's conversation plays appear to be written records of speech acts, and nothing more. They are not windows onto a nonlinguistic world. They are themselves the world—a world of conversations without stories.

A short play from this period, *Can You See the Name,* is one such conversation without a story:

CAN YOU SEE THE NAME

The name that I see is Howard.
Yes.
And the water that I see is the sea.
Yes.
And the land is the island.   5
Yes.
And the weather.
And the weather.
Cold
Indeed.   10
And the cause.
The cause of what.
The cause of lust.
Lust is not a name.
Indeed not.   15
And bushes.
Can you fear bushes.
Not I.
You mean you are braver.
Braver and braver.   20
What is the meaning of current.
Current topics.
Yes and then.
And then colors.
Green colors.   25
Lord Melbourne says blue is unlucky.
This is fear.
When can you see us.
Whenever I look.
And when are you careful.   30
I am very careful to smile.
Then we have our way.
Indeed you do and we wish it.
We are glad of your wishes.
It is not difficult to drive.   35
Curtain let us.
We do
We will.
Thank you so much.

You learnt that before.   40
I learn it again.
Do you know the difference in authors.[19]

Despite its brevity, *Can You See the Name* is typical in all other ways of
the longer conversation plays, most of which were published in *Geography and Plays*. In *Can You See the Name*, as in all of Stein's conversation plays, language is given prominence over, indeed, almost exists
without, the other components of theatrical art—objects, action, actors—which we are used to having suggested or called for in the dramatic text. We notice immediately, for example, the absence of a side
text; there are no stage directions, not even character ascriptions in
this play.[20] The more side text a play has, the more lines of the text
will have to be eliminated from performance, leaving gaps in the continuity of meaning or gaps in dramatic structure. These gaps will be
filled with action and with the dramatic space (including scenic set
and stage). Therefore, the more side text the playwright uses, the
more important action, actors, and space become, and conversely, the
less side text, the less important these elements are. In a play without
side text, the language is thus foregrounded.

The immediate effect of this foregrounding is to make the experience of reading this play similar in one respect to the experience
of hearing it recited. That is, for the reader of the play, as for the
auditor, all information about the objective world of the play must
come from the conversation. Naturally, the audience to a performance would also see objects and actions, but only those suggested by
the conversation (if the play had been faithfully staged). By this
foregrounding, our attention is drawn to the world-creating function
of dramatic dialogue, a function that distinguishes it from ordinary
discourse.

In creating the world of a play from its dialogue, we look for
objects and conditions, actors and actions specified by the dialogue.
Looking at *Can You See the Name* for "objects" we find a name, a sea,
an island, bushes, current topics, the color green, the color blue,
wishes, a curtain. As for conditions, we have cold weather, lust, fear,
bravery, carefulness, gladness, ease, difference. For actors, besides
the speakers (of which we may have two or more), we have a "Howard," a "Lord Melbourne," and some "authors." What do these actors
do? Some of them certainly talk, and when they talk, they use the
verbs "to look," "to see," "to smile," "to have one's way," "to drive,"
"to learn," and "to know." Nevertheless, beyond the scene setting of
the first section, the physical, objective, active world of the play is difficult to imagine because the things, conditions, actors, and actions I

have named, which are introduced as objects of discourse, remain forever in the world of discourse.

Stein's very title is emblematic of the way in which her play functions as an autonomous world of discourse without apparent connection to the world beyond the words. Ordinarily a play's title will evoke a central object, action, or condition that underlies all the talk of the play, for example, *The Wild Duck, Waiting for Godot,* or *Six Characters in Search of an Author.* But *Can You See the Name,* while it occupies the position of a title, is actually a line of the discourse, a question answered by the very first line: "The name that I see is Howard." This incorporation of the title into the conversation is a common device in Stein's conversation plays. In *Every Afternoon,* for example, the first line of the play is "I get up."[21] In *He Didn't Light the Light,* the play begins, "Go Right on / He didn't light his light. I mean he didn't yesterday. Or to-day either."[22]

It is not because of Stein's idiosyncratic use of titles alone that her plays are closed systems of discourse. It is also because of the words of the plays, specifically the nouns and verbs. The world of a play is specified through the nouns and verbs of the text. Stein's words themselves are sufficiently concrete, one would think, to fulfill the normal function of words in a play. The difference between Stein's play language and ordinary play language rests not in the kinds of words she chooses but in her use of them.

As in an ordinary play, the nouns in Stein's conversation plays are referential. So in line 3 of *Can You See the Name,* "And the water that I see is the sea," the noun "water" refers to an actual body of water which can be observed and which can be labeled with another noun, the near synonym "sea." But the noun "sea" is not only, nor most importantly, the sign of an object (a body of water) or of an event (looking at the body of water). It is itself both object and event. After all, water, the object, is first suggested in the conversation by the word "see" in the title and in line 1 (an object itself, a printed word on the page) which when spoken (when, that is, it becomes eventful) suggests its homonym "sea" which brings the object, the body of water, to mind. In other words, the noun "sea" has an undeniable connection to a physical entity, but its position and presentation in the conversation attenuate and de-emphasize its referentiality and emphasize instead its existence as a word suggested by another word which sounds the same but is spelled differently. In short, our attention is focused on phonology and orthography, not on meaning.[23]

With proper nouns, too, referentiality is de-emphasized. "Howard" may refer to a person, but in the world of this play, "Howard" is only a name that we can see, an object in the written text, an entity, not a referent. The name "Lord Melbourne," on the other hand, is clearly referring to someone, but this someone exists in the world of the play only as a topic of conversation, a name spoken and spoken about, part of a speech act, but not himself an actor.

In another conversation play the title of which is the proper noun "Mexico," we are repeatedly made aware of Stein's subversion of the referential meaning of this very specific place-name.[24] The word "Mexico" appears twenty-five times within the play, fulfilling three linguistic functions: it functions semantically as a place-name with specific conceptual associations; it functions syntactically as a noun with a definite grammatical role; and finally, it functions orthographically and phonologically when it appears without a semantic or syntactic context, as a word with a unique combination of letters.

"Mexico" refers to a geographical, historical, and cultural entity: the existence of a body of land, the creation of a nation, and the characteristics of that nation. Stein does not ignore the lexical meaning of "Mexico," nor does she disregard its nonlinguistic associations. She refers to its geographical boundaries: "Mexico tide water . . . Mexico border" (319); to its settlement as a colony of Spain: "If there is a Mallorcan name if Mallorca gave the missionary who converted the California settlers if the Mallorcans have a little town of their own near New York then we will believe in Spanish influence in Mexico. The Spaniards are not liked in Mexico" (325); to its language: "Mexico is prettily pronounced in Spanish" (306); to its agriculture: "Do dates grow in Mexico. They do somewhere. Not the edible kind. No not the edible kind" (315); and to its cities: "This is the right city of Mexico. / Or street of Mexico. / Street of Mexico" (308). Thus, "Mexico" is not an abstraction. The word specifies a physical entity, but once it enters the conversation, its attachment to that entity is attenuated. Its concrete associations are not eliminated, but neither are they emphasized.

Thus, in the first example cited, the references to the Gulf of Mexico and to the Mexican border, set in context, read:

Mexico tide water. I meant not to spell it so.
Mexico tied water.
Mexico border.
I love the letters m and o. (319)

Orthography is a more important preoccupation here than geography. "Mexico" is as much a word being written into a text as it is a nation.[25]

"Mexico" is also a spoken word, the subject of a conversation, not that the conversation is "about Mexico," but that the word itself is the syntactical subject of many of the statements in the conversation. The conversation might just as well be about Bolivia, Argentina, or the United States. Indeed, the substitution of another place-name for "Mexico" would create hardly a ripple in the conversation. The word's specific reference is almost irrelevant.

Since it is a place-name, "Mexico" functions grammatically as a noun. In sentences where meaningful reference is incompatible with correct grammar, grammar prevails. Because it is a noun, "Mexico" can be modified by an adjective, as in "a little Mexico" (309), and can be the object of a preposition as in "Don't please me with Mexico" (322). In both examples "Mexico" is used correctly according to the rules of grammar. However, grammar links "Mexico" to words which are semantically inappropriate. As the name of a unique country, "Mexico" does not come in various sizes. Nor can we please someone with a thing over which we have no control or power. The speaker might please the listener with a trip to Mexico or a gift from Mexico, or even, and especially, with the word "Mexico," but not with Mexico itself. In these instances, then, "Mexico" is clearly functioning as a part of speech rather than as a name with specific reference.

By far the most frequent use of "Mexico" in this play is as an isolated word without contextual significance, as in the following example:

> Mexico.
> Mexico is prettily pronounced in Spanish.
> Pronounce it for me.
> Yes I will.
> Say it prettily.
> Mexico. (306)

Here, the word "Mexico" appears first and last as a word, the word which is the title of the play and a word which is spoken in the play. When "Mexico" is isolated and presented as an object to be seen and a sound to be heard, its referential significance is of minor importance. "Mexico" is not only, nor most importantly, the sign of an entity or event. As a word "Mexico" is itself both entity and event. Whether Stein uses nouns as subjects, or as subjects of sentences, or simply as words, she forces us to concentrate on language, not to look through it.

The frequent recurrence of the word "Mexico" in the play *Mexico* is the exception rather than the rule in the conversation plays. More often than not, a noun, once introduced, may never reappear. This further subverts the normal functioning of dramatic dialogue which is distinguished from normal discourse by a high degree of co-referentiality, an interconnectedness of the objects of discourse.[26] Ordinarily, with each appearance, by a process of accretion, the object becomes something more than the word it was in its first appearance as an object of discourse. This process by which a word acquires attributes beyond its lexical meaning, its grammatical function, its spelling, and its pronunciation does not take place in Stein's conversation plays.

Like her nouns, Stein's verbs function to keep the objects of discourse in the world of discourse. An inventory of Stein's verbs as they occur throughout the conversation plays helps to explain how they accomplish this. Of the thirty verbs in *Can You See the Name*, for example, one-third are forms of the verb "to be." This ratio holds true in most of the conversation plays. Stein also favors verbs which express preference—"care for," "like," and "wish," for instance—or which express a mental activity—"know," "remember," "learn," "understand," "recollect," and "forget." These types of verbs do not suggest nonlinguistic actions that might accompany the conversation in which they occur.

The most common verbs in the conversation plays are metalingual verbs: mean, hear, explain, mention, speak, say, assure, ask, agree, call, contradict, promise, pronounce, and spell.[27] Thus, the most common activities in these plays are naming, describing, and speaking—all linguistic activities. All of these linguistic activities occur within the primary activity, conversation.

True action verbs, when they occur, are often presented in inactive forms: in the infinitive—"It is not difficult to drive"; "I am very careful to smile" (*Can You See the Name*); "I consider that it is not necessary for me to teach languages";[28] or with the auxiliary "can"—"Can you fear bushes"; "When can you see us" (*Can You See the Name*); "I can supply furs";[29] "Can you laugh at me";[30] "You can regulate your expenditure"[31]—all suggesting the possibility of action but not action itself.

Action verbs presented actively are primarily presented as responses to questions, not as responses to actions that have just occurred in the world of the play. For example:

What did you do with your dog.
We sent him into the country.
Was he a trouble.
Not at all but we thought he would be better off there.

Yes it isn't right to keep a large dog in the city.
Yes I agree with you.
Yes[32]

Action exists most frequently, then, outside the world of the play and exists at all only because it is reported in the "here and now" of the dialogue.[33]

Stein does use two active verb forms, the future and the imperative (a voice that is a kind of future tense, since the action commanded in the here and now of utterance will be done at some future moment). We can imagine staging the events called for in Stein's future tense and imperative sentences. For example, in the play *Every Afternoon* the statement, "We will go and hear Tito Ruffo," could lead a director to stage a recital at which the speakers might hear the singing of an actor playing the Italian baritone. However, the text itself tells us that the activity of hearing Tito Ruffo is subsidiary to the activity of punning on the word "hear":

We will go and hear Tito Ruffo.
Here.
Yes here.
Oh yes I remember about that. He is to be here.[34]

The action, "hearing," and its complementary action, "singing," are only future possibilities discussed by the speakers. Here, in this text, during this conversation which the audience hears, the punning on the word "hear" is the only action.

Furthermore, the few future tense and imperative actions suggested in conversation are not sustained beyond the moment of their singular utterance. We hear nothing further about Tito Ruffo in *Every Afternoon*. Even when an action is mentioned repeatedly, like the command "Count her dresses" in the play *Counting Her Dresses*, its recurrences are much like those of the word "Mexico" in that play. The words are repeated, but the repetitions serve to fragment the text rather than to join its parts. No connection is made between separate occurrences. The repeated words and phrases do not recur at regular intervals, or in the same or similar contexts, or with the same or similar reference. Instead of unifying the whole, such repetition interrupts the ongoing flow of the whole, constantly sending the listener back to a new beginning. We never see in Stein's conversation plays the progressive construction of a coherent text or a coherent world. Stein imposes no temporal ordering and no action structure on the few true actions her speakers mention in their conversations.

So it is that Stein's verbs and the uses she makes of them work against the characteristic of dramatic dialogue which J. L. Styan has called "the primacy of the occasion"[35] and Keir Elam has identified as "the primary allegiance of language in the drama" to the "course of events."[36] Stein's plays emphasize the primacy of language; her conversations follow no other course than the democratic turn-taking of social discourse.

In the social discourse recorded in *Can You See the Name*, the speaking partners behave as collaborators in the clarification of meaning and the amplification of information to their own satisfaction. Yet their conversation is not clear and informative for the reader/spectator's purposes because it has the characteristics of ordinary social discourse—"digression, redundancies, non sequiturs, sudden changes of topic and ... an overall inconclusiveness"—characteristics that make ordinary discourse much less clear and informative than dramatic dialogue.[37] In *Can You See the Name* the speakers change the topic abruptly at lines 13, 16, 21, 24, 27, 28, 30, 35, 36, 40, and 42. Almost every change of topic is a non sequitur; there is no strategic organization at work in this conversation. Some topics recur: "fear," introduced in line 17, is reintroduced in line 27; "seeing," the topic that initiates the conversation, appears again in line 28. But these repetitions do nothing to develop the topic. They contribute, in fact, to the overall inconclusiveness and fragmentation of this conversation which begins and ends with a question. Despite the confusion such a conversation causes the reader/spectator, the speakers appear to understand each other quite well. This play, then, is truly a closed world, one constituted as if there were no outside observers. Compared to this play, so-called realistic drama with its invisible fourth wall can be seen more clearly as the artifact it is, an artifact constructed from the natural materials of dialogic exchange which are then strategically manipulated to inform and to affect the eventual audience at the performance. Stein's plays subvert the informational and affective function of dramatic dialogue. They are dialogic exchanges, but in them, the give-and-take of dialogue is not shaped by considerations of plot, performance, or even character.

The participants in this social discourse are not at all like the characters who emerge from most dramatic dialogue. In the first place, the lines of dialogue are undifferentiated from speaker to speaker, leading some to believe, as Richard Bridgman does, that they issue "from a single sensibility."[38] Of course, all the words in any play text issue from a single sensibility, the dramatist's, but ordinarily we expect the dramatist to manipulate language so that it appears to issue from several sensibilities since one of the chief functions of

dramatic dialogue is to create characters that actors can then impersonate.[39] Like all plays, Stein's are imagined as being uttered by more
than one speaker. The absence of idiosyncrasies differentiating one
speaker from the next points to the absence, not of speakers, but of
characters. Language is foregrounded and characters, like objects,
conditions, and actions, are de-emphasized.

Even when speakers are named, as they are in a few of the conversation plays, and even when they give us information about themselves, they are not characters. The following excerpt from *Please Do
Not Suffer* has named speakers and gives us some information about
these speakers:

> (Genevieve.) I like to choose my meat.
> (Mrs. Marchand.) I understand everything better. I like to have to
> think and look at maps. I hate to see so much black. I do not mean
> by that that I am sullen. I am not that. I am delighted with sur-
> roundings.
> (Genevieve.) I wish to spend a little money on some things. I am
> waiting for the boat. I have nothing to do except sleep. Really not.
> (Mrs. Marchand.) I understand Spanish.
> (Count Daisy Wrangel.) To please him and to please me I do not
> dine at home.[40]

In order for Mrs. Marchand to be a character, the information she
gives us throughout the play would have to cohere. Susanne Langer
has stated that "a character [in a play] stands before us as a coherent
whole."[41] This Stein's speakers never do. That Mrs. Marchand hates
to see so much black, is delighted with her surroundings, and understands Spanish are unconnected bits of information about her. There
is no point to our remembering them because they will remain dis-
crete fragments and will never be connected to other fragments yet
to come in the play. Therefore, despite the overtly self-reflexive content of their speeches, Stein's speakers are not characterized, either
by habits of speech or through coherent portrayal.

In Stein's plays conversation and characterization appear to be
mutually exclusive. In the two plays from this period with consistent
speaker ascriptions—*Please Do Not Suffer* and *Do Let Us Go Away*—
conversation all but disappears. Speakers address us, but they do not
address each other. Quite often their speeches are delivered in the
third person and seem more like descriptions of the person whose
name precedes them than statements by that person, as in the following example from *Please Do Not Suffer*:

William and Mary.

(William.) He is fond of reading and drinking. He drinks wine. He also drinks siphon. This is water with sterilised water in it. He drinks it with and also without lemon. He is very fond of walking. He does not prefer resting. He is a painter by profession.
(Mary.) Mary is winning. She has a brother who is fighting. He has made a ring for her. She has a mother and another brother. We were asked does she like swimming. She has not a knowledge of swimming. (264)

This is not conversation; this is a kind of portraiture in which the speakers recite the author's portraits of them. Even when they use the first person, the speakers in *Please Do Not Suffer* are using speech for self-description, as Genevieve does in the following:

(Genevieve.) She believes in Fraconville. What is a thunder storm. This is my history. I worked at a cafe in Rennes. Before that I was instructed by a woman who knew knitting and everything. My mother and father worked at gardening. I was ruined by a butcher. I am not particularly fond of children. My child is a girl and is still a little one. She is living in an invaded district but is now in Avignon. I had a coat made for her but it did not fit her very well and now I am sending the money so that it will be made at Verdun. I am not necessarily a very happy woman. Every one is willing. (262–263)

Since all but the first two statements are self-involved, they elicit and receive no response. The concatenated address/response of conversation is missing. These speakers speak into a void. They may be heard, but they are not acknowledged. This is true even when named speakers are not being self-descriptive. For instance:

(Mildred.) It is copied. Six handkerchiefs. Two of one kind four of another.
(Carrie.) She backhands that means she takes good care of herself.
(Mrs. Marchand.) She does not know any of them. She knows Mr. Rothschild.
(Genevieve.) What is the use of being tranquil when this house is built for the winter. The winter here is warm. (264)

We know this is conversation only because Stein has ascribed it to different speakers. Since the statements of the speakers are juxtaposed on the printed page, we assume that they are speaking to each other, but nothing in what they say supports this assumption.

In *Do Let Us Go Away* Stein even has one of the speakers say, "Oh I am disgusted. This is not the conversation," after he has participated in the following "exchange":

> (Jane and Nicholas and Theodore and the lawyer and the children.)
> (Jane.) I speak slowly. I do it intentionally.
> (Henry.) We have fragments. We call out sometimes. When two bands are playing they play in the distance. Some play in people's houses. We say hush.
> (Arthur.) Dishonored. Never believe in September. Never believe in September in the sense of visions.
> (Henry.) I do know the chorus. Individual cases do not bring the war home to me. I suddenly remember and I rest in it. I am ashamed. I have patience and earnest feeling. I am liking the new boat. It is still painted white and is enormously disappointing. Some one has been willing. Oh I am disgusted. This is not the conversation.[42]

A conversation requires not only that there be speakers but also that there be a verbal connection between those speakers.

In *Please Do Not Suffer* a conversation is temporarily established at the very end of the play when the succession of self-reflexive statements by named speakers is interrupted by unascribed responses:

> (Harry Francis.) It hangs out in the rain and it is not dry what shall I put on underneath.
> > Anything you like.
> (Roger Henry.) Why do you prefer a picture of a boat.
> > Because it is useful.
> (Mrs. Marchand.) I am so disappointed in the morning.
> > We are all of us disappointed.
> (Mrs. Marchand.) I did not meet you to-day.
> > Yes you did.
> > Every man swallowing. What.
> (Mrs. Marchand.) I told you that you had every reason to expect warm weather and now it's cold.
> > It won't be cold long I hope. These are equinoxial storms.
> > They last from seven to ten days. (266)

The unnamed speaker introduces the pronoun "you" and uses the collective "we." He/she is the only speaker who responds to the state-

ments of the others, thereby giving the named speakers the opportunity to address their remarks to someone.[43]

Turkey and Bones and Eating and We Liked It and *For the Country
Entirely,* two plays which combine ascribed and unascribed sections,
make a similar connection between namelessness and successful conversation. The unascribed portions are conversations; the ascribed
portions are simply collections of self-definitive statements. A name
set a person apart from other people, and each time that person is
defined or described, he is set still further apart. In Stein's conversation plays, conversation and characterization are incompatible. As far
as Stein was concerned, "drama" only occurs when characterization is
abandoned.

The drama in Stein's conversation plays is in the language. It is
in the speech acts and the relationships they establish. It is in the way
the speakers collaborate through language. It is in the momentum of
the language, the rhythms of social discourse. It is in the suggestive-
ness of words, how they can trigger a thought and change the subject
of the conversation. Because the plays emphasize language by placing
it at the apex of the performance hierarchy and by minimizing or
eliminating the other components of theatrical art, they force us to
concentrate on the drama inherent in language, independent of its
connection to objects, actions, and actors. In fact, they suggest that
there is no nonlinguistic world, that the world exists only when word
of it is written or uttered.

Let us imagine for a moment what would happen to these play
texts in performance.[44] Stein was not writing closet drama or literary
dialogues. She intended her plays to be performed.[45] In performance, the language of the play is given voice. If the play text is a
conversation, then that conversation will be performed by speakers.
Once language becomes attached to living people, the playwright
loses control of it as a medium. Speech becomes identified with the
individual who utters it. No matter how assiduously the playwright
avoids characterization, speech is a characterizing act. By imitating
conversation and by foregrounding it, Stein was automatically creating an opportunity for the speaker to mimic a living person and
through the tone, intensity, and timbre of his voice to invest that person with character. Since actors have bodies as well as voices, they will
"act" as well as speak. Keir Elam writes: "The language of the drama
calls for the intervention of the actor's body in the completion of its
meanings. Its corporality is essential rather than an optional extra."[46]
At the very least an actor will normally underline speech with acces-
sory movement, gestures, and the like.

A performance that is true to the text of these plays will minimize characterization and action. Nonetheless, in even the most

impersonal and static performance, the very components of theatrical art which Stein's plays eliminate or "demote" can reenter the play through the intermediary of the actor. Because Stein's medium is conversation, the autonomy and primacy of language will inevitably be compromised in performance, no matter how faithful that performance is to the written text. The conflict between the written play text and the performance text (in which all the elements that the written text eliminated become reinstated) eventually replaces conversation as the source of the drama in Stein's plays.

Chapter 2

The Play as Lang-scape: 1920 to 1933

The plays collected in *Operas and Plays* and *Last Operas and Plays*, written between 1920 and 1933, Gertrude Stein called landscapes. I have adapted rather than adopted her term partly because there is no evidence that the desire to create verbal landscapes guided her in the writing of these plays. She first called her plays landscapes in her 1935 lecture "Plays," well after most of them had been written. Moreover, "landscape" is less than satisfactory as a descriptive designation of these plays because it suggests that they represent, evoke, or in some manner correspond to a specific place (an idea Stein fosters with her claim that they were inspired by the countryside around Bilignin—as was the novel *Lucy Church Amiably*). In fact, the plays are not about Bilignin nor about any other place. Rather, they are about language and its relationship to the performance event; they are about writing for the theater, thus, my alteration of the prefix—from "land" to "lang"—to give some sense of the true subject of these plays. Although "landscape" does not adequately describe the plays, I did not wish to abandon the term entirely, for I find landscape a suggestive metaphor for Stein's plays. I therefore wanted to retain some trace of it.

The metaphoric connection between landscape and theater has a long tradition, embodied most neatly in the word "scene" with its application to both worlds. In the essay "Thought and Landscape," Yi-Fu Tuan defines landscape as a "space in which people *act*," or "*scenery* for people to contemplate" (emphasis added).[1] In the same spirit, but centuries earlier, theater was "a word much used in the titles of books of travel and [geographic] description," according to John Brinckerhoff Jackson.[2] On the other side of the metaphoric field, dramatists of the sixteenth and seventeenth centuries made frequent use of the *theatrum mundi* topos, and during the same period, the Italians developed the proscenium stage which borrowed its vanishing point perspective and disposition of loci in space from landscape painting. In choosing this metaphor for her own plays, then, Stein reminds us of a centuries-old theatrical convention.

Although Stein's plays are not in themselves landscapes, not the verbal depiction or evocation of a scene, they are like landscapes. The similitude lies in Stein's use of language. About the similarity between landscape and language, John Jakle writes, "Landscapes comprise a syntax. Not only do objects have meaning like words, but objects relate spatially not unlike a grammatical structure. Objects in the environment can have collective meaning given the visual relationships of place."[3] Stein treats her words as though they are material objects related to each other spatially, that is, visually on the page and sonorously in the air. Her language assumes a materiality equal in presence to the materiality of the other elements of the performance event.

Furthermore, the effect of these plays on our perception of their performance is similar to the effect of landscape on our perception of our environment. Originally an Anglo-Saxon word which meant simply a tract of land, "landscape" fell out of use until it was revived by Dutch painters in 1600 to refer to their representations of a scene. "Landscape" in its modern usage, then, described first a kind of painting and only later the view or prospect itself.[4] The word as a designation of something in the environment, the view we see, would always suggest artfulness. As Jackson writes, landscape "is *always* artificial." It is always a composition, whether created as such by a landscape architect or organized that way by the eye of the perceiver, trained by art to compose the view.[5] A word like "landscape," which suggests the power of art to alter perception, has a wonderful resonance when applied to Stein's plays because their structure, their "scape," alters the normal course of the theater event. By opposing the dynamism of actor and action, Stein's plays create a kind of verbal stasis within theater time, much as a landscape painting frames and freezes a visual moment in natural time or as a "real" landscape interferes with the process of nature.[6] Within this stasis, Stein represents an event not normally represented in the theater: the writing of the play.

These phenomena, these landscaping activities performed with language, will be the subject of this chapter, which will focus on two representative plays: *A List* (1923), in which the primary concern is with the spatiality of the theater, and *Four Saints in Three Acts* (1927), in which the primary concern is with the temporality of the theater.

I

In *A List*, as in other lang-scape plays written between 1920 and 1923, the words of the play are presented first and foremost as visible objects, the writer's materials. How they look on the page (spelling, capitalization, physical placement) and how they relate to each other (punctuation and syntax) determine how the theater event will be constituted. Thus, Stein asserts the spatiality of words and the primacy of the written text (both side text and main text) over the performance text. Far from making her written text the transparent instrument of theatrical realization, she makes it a material presence whose existence and contours are the subject of debate and discussion within the play. The actors in a Stein play are never allowed to forget that their own material existence depends upon a particular reading of the written text. The theater event of which a Stein play is a part really begins with that reading, with the encounter between enactor (producer, director, or actor) and text. Lawrence Kornfeld, the director of a number of Stein's plays, has described his and his actors' encounters with Stein's texts:

For me, the real play is the process. . . . Gertrude Stein's plays can be very boring if the director tries to make them all about the words of ideas, or the words of love, or the words of painting or the words about words. This is wrong. The director must fight the plays and then he will find out what the words mean, not what the words are about. Only Gertrude Stein knew what the words were about; we can manage to hear what they mean if we put up a good fight. Only Gertrude Stein cared what the words were about and maybe some of her friends for gossip cared, but I only care about what they will mean after we all fight over them.[7]

When we look at *A List*, we can see how a Stein play engages its enactors in a "fight" as they try to move from reading to enactment. In a conventional play the side text exists to facilitate enactment. Each name in the side text signifies a new "character" which the actor will then impersonate in performance. The establishment of a character list is, thus, a fairly straightforward affair (often done for the actors by the playwright in a list that precedes the first act of the play). By contrast, the side text in *A List* presents an immediate challenge. In this play which Stein teasingly calls *A List*, a list of characters is not, in fact, very easy to generate.

In Stein's notational system a name followed by a period is a character speaking:

    Martha.   not interesting.

Two names joined by "and" signifies two characters speaking in unison:

    Martha
      and   Included.
    Maryas.

Three names, three characters:

    Mabel
    Martha
      and   Various re-agents make me see victoriously.
    Maryas.

What are we to make, then, of this configuration?

    Mabel
    Martha
      and   Susan Mabel Martha and Susan, Mabel and Martha
    Mabel   and a father.
      and   There was no sinking there, there where there was
    Martha.   no placid carrier.[8]

Do we have two characters, Mabel and Martha, or three characters, Mabel Martha, and Mabel, and Martha? We have only two names after all, but the usual correspondence between name and person is disrupted here by the arrangement of the names and their relationship via the connector "and." The words spoken by this group of characters further emphasize the effect of syntax on meaning. When they say "Susan Mabel Martha and Susan, Mabel and Martha" the same names appear on both sides of that first "and." In performance this line would sound like the repetition of names referring to the same people. But the written text gives us different information because of the existence of the comma. (The inclusion of "and" between "Mabel" and "Martha" also alters the significance of the three names.) We cannot "recognize it by the name" as one of the characters later challenges us to do, partly because the meaning of a name—or of any word—can be altered by its syntactical placement, not only within a sentence or a phrase, but also within the play.[9]

The title of this play, for example, is "A List." This configuration of words means that there is only one list unless, as happens halfway into the play, we encounter the same words arranged like this:

LIST A

By a syntactical reversal, the single list becomes the first of a number of lists—but only in the side text, for within the main text (the text to be spoken) the characters continue to refer exclusively to "a list." Meaning then depends on where words (names) appear within the grammar of the sentence and within the grammar of the text.

When the characters begin referring to a second list, the existence of more than a single list enters the world of the main text. Yet the main text stops with a second list, while the side text gives us "THIRD LIST," "FOURTH LIST," "LIST FIVE," and "A LAST LIST." Six lists in all, or seven if we count the first list announced by the title of the play, but six or seven only within that part of the composition which is the side text, six or seven lists only for the reader not for the spectator or listener. If we are to recognize it by the name, our recognition will depend upon what field of composition we are attending to. If we want to recognize all of "it" in a play, we must look at the written text as well as listen to the performance text.

Moreover, we must look at the written text, too, because only there can we see the words spelled out for us. Through an abundance of homophones, homonyms, and puns, Stein demonstrates how difficult it is to get a fix on the material world of the play without first getting a fix on the material of the play—those letters out of which spelling makes recognizable names. Only when we can see the words can we understand what we are hearing in performance.

Take, for example, the character names, Maryas and Marius. As written they are distinguishable, and so, in the side text, they seem to stand for two separate characters (except when they combine as in the "Mabel Martha" mode discussed above). But Maryas and Marius are near-homophones and when spoken they are barely distinguishable. If both names are pronounced the same, what then becomes of the two characters signaled by the names? This is a question which naturally concerns not only the eventual actors but the "characters" themselves.[10] Marius asks, "How do you spell Marius" because his very existence depends on the spelling of his name in the written text (96). In the following exchange the characters meditate on the difference between speaking and spelling:

Maryas and Martha.	More Maryas and more Martha.
Maryas and Martha.	More Martha and more Maryas.
Martha and Maryas.	More and more and more Martha and more Maryas.
Marius.	It is spoken of in that way.
Mabel.	It is spoken of in that way.
Marius and Mabel.	It is spoken in that way and it is spoken of in that way.
Marius and Mabel.	It is spoken of in that way.
Mabel.	I speak of it in that way.
Marius.	I have spoken of it in that way and I speak it in that way. I have spoken of it in that way.
Mabel.	I speak of it in that way.
Mabel.	Spelled in this way.
Marius.	Spelled in that way.
Mabel.	Spelled in this way and spelled in that way and spoken of in this way and spoken of in that way and spoken in this way. (93)

The other characters speak of "Maryas," but when they speak of him, the names which are spelled in this way—"Maryas"—and in that way—"Marius"—might be spoken in only one way. When we hear the words in performance we may hear only one name unless the actors take great care to pronounce the two names differently. We must attend to the written text in order to compose an accurate list of characters.

Stein plays further with the names "Maryas" and "Marius" when she introduces characters named May and Mary. In the main text Stein puns on these character names and shows that orthography and syntax (textual matters) can change a speaker into a word spoken and can make characters difficult to recognize by their names. May, a character named once in the side text, is never referred to by name; however, her name appears often in the main text as the auxiliary verb "may."

Martha.   One may say that one may say that a brother tardily
             marries.
Maryas.   In this way. (99)

Not only is "may" a pun on the name "May," but also "marries"
is "in this way" a pun on Maryas. Stein also puns on the name Mary.
Spelled with two "r's" and a lowercase "m," Mary becomes "marry";
May and Mary together become in the main text "may marry."

Mary.   Mary may no I may say may Mary. . . .
             . . . .
May.   And Mary.
Martha
Mabel
Maryas
   and   We may marry. (103)
Mary.

Another pun on "Mary" occurs when Martha and Maryas say,
"We translate this into that and Mary is so gracious and Mary" (97).
They are referring to the new character Mary, but they are also punning on the name of the character who is speaking (Mary is/Maryas)
and on the name of another character (Marius). There are ortho-
graphical differences between May/may, Mary/marry, marries/Mar-
yas/Marius/Mary is. We can see when we read the text that these
words are "translations," that is, transfigurations rather than exact
transcriptions, but the distinctions among the words would blur in
performance.[11]
    That the written text is more reliable than the performance text
as a key to exactly what is said and what is seen is further emphasized
with the appearance of other homophones within the main text. For
example, Maryas poses the following number puzzle:

Sixteen if sixteen carry four, four more, if five more carry four for
more if four more carry four, if four carry fifty more, if four more
five hundred and four and for more than that, and four more than
eighty four. Four more can carry sixteen if you please if it is acceptable. (91)

When we hear the word "four," we will correctly assume because of
its context that we are hearing the particular sequence of letters that

signifies the number 4. However, we will also assume, this time incorrectly, that "for" means the number 4. Only the written text can set us straight.

In the following sequence, too, the written text has more authority than the performance text:

Maryas.	Not too long.
Maryas and Martha.	Not too long.
Maryas.	To long and to long.
Martha.	To long.
Maryas.	Able to long able to be and to be safely to be safely able to be safely to be safely to be seen to be seen able to long to be safely to safely be here and there to be there. Able to be there. To long. Who is longing now. (94)

It is only by reading the written text that we can see when "too" changes to "to" and therefore when "long" changes from an adjective to a verb, from one meaning to another. The spelling of a word in the text determines not only its own meaning but the meaning of contiguous words.

Names, however, are not like the words "to" and "for." Names (and by extension, nouns) have a correspondence to something in the material world. (Names and nouns can also stand for ideas and abstractions, but Stein is more concerned here with the relationship between a name and an object). Maryas Mabel and Martin ask, "How are you known," and answer, "You are known by your name and your share" (102). Or as Martha later puts it, "Carrots and artichokes marguerites and roses. If you can repeat it and somebody chose it, somebody shows it, somebody knows it. If you can repeat and somebody knows it" (103). Objects are known by their names and by their "share," their unique place in the material world. The name is that which was chosen to represent a unique carrot, a particular rose. We repeat the name and each time we do "carrot" is shown and carrot is known. This is a very generalized carrot, not the first one seen when someone chose the name for it. The name is not exactly the same thing as each and every carrot that has a share in the material universe, but the name is one way to recognize the existence of carrot.

So it is when we make a list; the names on it have a direct correspondence to items with a share in the world. Either we make a list of what we see—a list of the contents of a box, for instance, in which case we write down a name for each item we pull out of the box. Or we make a list of what we wish to see or what we believe we could eventually see—a shopping list, for example, in which case we are certain that for each name we write down there exists an item that can be procured by the person who takes the shopping list to the appropriate place.

This is not exactly the situation with a character list, however. The names on a character list do not correspond to anything or anyone preexisting in the material world. The names are inventions of the dramatist that correspond to imagined beings who exist only in the private world of the dramatist's mind. (This is even true, to a certain extent, of characters with the names of historical personages.) To make a list of characters, then, we must look to the dramatist, not to the visible world.

The problem of making such a list in *A List* is first posed by Martha as a meditation that becomes a leitmotif of the play:

| Martha. | If four are sitting at a table and one of them is lying upon it it does not make any difference. If bread and pomegranates are on a table and four are sitting at the table and one of them is leaning upon it it does not make any difference. |
| Martha. | It does not make any difference if four are seated at a table and one is leaning upon it. (92) |

Bread and pomegranates, having been named and having names which correspond to real objects, can be said without hesitation to be on the table. But what can be said for certain about the people sitting at the table? Without names they are at the mercy of syntax. One of them can appear and disappear with the shifting of a few words. If we say, "four are sitting at the table and one of them is leaning upon it," we are speaking of four people, but if we eliminate the phrase "of them" and say that four are seated and one is leaning, we may now be speaking of either four or five people. If Stein had written unequivocally, "Martha and Mabel and Martin and Marius are sitting at the table and Mary is leaning upon it," we would know how many people are at the table.

Or would we? "Yes and know" to borrow a line from the play. As we have seen, even when we move out into the side text, a space full of names, we meet with a writer who teases us with her homophones and her syntactical maneuvers, teases us with the essentially self-contained world of the written text where words exist not as pointers but as objects in a composition. In this play, as Martha says, "the pansy is a bird as well as a flower rice is a bird as well as a plant, cuckoo is a flower as well as a bird" (91). Whatever correspondence the words have to a material world beyond the play, that correspondence is not the only, and certainly not the most important reason for their presence in the play.

The experience Lawrence Kornfeld and his actors have had with Stein's plays is an experience I believe Stein intended them to have. Stein's language does not represent something else. It simply exhibits itself. The enactor's first act must be to experience the language and not to read into it a meaning that the text does not itself present. By opposing the processes an enactor would normally go through to dissolve, transform, overwhelm, menace, or subordinate the written text in order to create the performance text, Stein asserts the substantiality of her written text and makes it an active participant, as it were, in the process of its own enactment.

Let us suppose, now, that an enactor has met Stein's challenge and has created from the written text of *A List*, a performance text that is to be exhibited to an audience. Even in the performance text, language is foregrounded, is made "conspicuous."[12] What is conspicuous in the performance of *A List* (or what would be conspicuous—the play has not, to my knowledge, been performed) is not of course the way words look but the way words sound. As sonorous objects the words in *A List* do not differ that much from the words in other non-dramatic Stein texts of the same period, except insofar as the words here are meant to be spoken aloud.

Here, as elsewhere, Stein makes use of repetition to throw words into relief:

Martha.   If on a day that comes again and if we consider a day a week day it does come again if on a day that comes again and we consider every day to be a day that comes again it comes again then when accidentally when very accidentally every other day and every other day every other day and every other day that comes again and every day comes again when accidentally every other day comes again, every other day comes again and every other and every day comes again and accidentally and every day and it comes again, a day comes again and a day in that way comes again.

Maryas.   Accidentally in the morning and after that every evening and accidentally every evening and after that every morning and after that accidentally every morning and after that accidentally and after that every morning. (92)

The first sounds we hear distinguished from the ongoing flow of words by repetition are those of the phrase "comes again" and the word "day." The reverberation of "comes again" and "day" continues until the word "accidentally" is introduced. This word is also repeated, less frequently than "day" and "comes again," and less euphoniously than "comes again" because of all the dentals in the word. If this were a musical composition, one might imagine "accidentally" as a percussive sound. The next phrase the ear can distinguish is "every other day," repeated in rapid succession and then united with "comes again." The two phrases, with occasional interruption from "accidentally," will play out together till the end of Martha's speech. Maryas picks up on the percussive word "accidentally" and begins with it a speech that repeats and combines the words "accidentally," "every morning," and "every evening" in a more staccato rhythm than we heard in Martha's speech.

The words are repeated but modulated by combining with other words. The repetition calls our attention to the sounds of words; the modulation to their playfulness. In performance, these aesthetic qualities of language would be insistent, making it difficult for us to attend to other qualities like instrumentality and reference. *A List* is not about morning or evening or days or accidents. If these words mean anything, they might refer to private concerns of the writer, but in performance, reference remains private and inconsequential. The metadramatic content of the written text is also not apparent in performance. What we have in performance is sound. We might try to draw meaning from the words, but our attention to them as signifiers would be distracted by our awareness of them as objects "filling" the air of the theater as sound can fill a room.

The sonority of Stein's text comes not only from repetition but also from rhyme: "A single instance of able to pay any day and as you say" (91); from near rhyme: "Exchange challenges for challenges and by and by defy, and define by and by Battling Siki and so high. He is higher than they say. You know why beads are broader, in order to be in order to be an order to be strung together" (90); from alliteration: "Change songs for safety, change their songs for their safety. Safely change their songs" (94); from assonance and consonance: "And if they were in various ways differently decided, and if they were delighted, no not delighted, and if they were accidentally relieved and repeatedly received and reservedly deceived, if they were separately announced and deposed and respectfully recalled and regularly preceeded, indeed they were there indeed they were there" (94–95); and by a constant interplay of these devices—as all the examples demonstrate.

In *A List* the speeches of characters are not connected conversationally, but chorally. For example:

Martha.	And forget her.
Maryas.	And respect him.
Marius.	And neglect them.
Mabel.	And they collect them as lilies of the valley in this country. (90–91)

Or:

Marius and Mabel.	Please to please. Pleasure to give pleasure.
Marius.	To please and to give pleasure.
Marius and Mabel.	To please and please and to give pleasure and to to give pleasure.
Marius.	To please and to give pleasure.
Marius and Mabel.	If you please if you please and if you give pleasure.
Marius.	If you give pleasure and if you please.
Marius and Mabel.	Please please and pleasure.
Marius.	I am very pleased I am indeed very pleased that it is a great pleasure. (92)

These characters seldom use language as an instrument of communication. Rather than responding to what the words mean, they simply respond to the words. They repeat them, or they repeat them with slight variations. They match the sounds of words already spoken with similar sounds, like poets completing each other's poems. They free-associate in a world where words suggest other words.

This foregrounding of "phonetic formations," what Roman Ingarden has identified as the fundamental stratum, "essential constituent," and "indispensable element" of the literary work of art, is also a metadramatic activity.[13] By giving prominence to language sounds, Stein is calling attention to the materials from which the play has been constructed. She is making opaque that which is usually transparent. By subverting the conventional role of dramatic language in this way, Stein is making the spectator attend to the materiality of language, to its existence as an aesthetic object. Calderwood calls this particular metatextual stance the "lyric impulse"—the impulse "to construct a self-enclosed verbal context indifferent to outside realities and concerned less to communicate meanings than to exploit them autistically."[14]

There are, of course, certain drawbacks to this lyric impulse, especially when it is indulged in by someone writing for the theater. Stein herself acknowledged both the attraction and the danger of this kind of writing when she discussed the writing of this period in her 1935 lecture on her literary portraits:

> I found that I was for a little while very much taken with the beauty of the sounds as they came from me as I made them.
> This is a thing that may be at any time a temptation. This temptation came to me a little after the Saint Remy period when I wrote Saints in Seven, Four Religions, Capital Capitals. . . . [it] resulted in . . . an extraordinary melody of words and a melody of excitement in knowing that I had done this thing.
> . . . This melody for a little while after rather got the better of me. . . . I did begin to think that I was rather drunk with what I had done. And I am always one to prefer being sober. I must be sober. It is so much more exciting to be sober, to be exact and concentrated and sober. So then as I say I began again.[15]

The intoxication of melody, the sheer aesthetic bliss of it, can turn to mindless drunkenness if the lyric impulse is allowed to overwhelm all other impulses. Language can become nonsense if it is deprived completely of referential meaning. As Keir Elam writes, "The free play of the signifiers rapidly becomes a semiotic straightjacket."[16]

It is impossible to say whether or not Stein realized in 1922 the limitations of linguistic free play in a performance text. The fact is, though, that Stein wrote no plays from 1923 to 1927. Richard Bridgman has explained that from 1923 to 1925 *The Making of Americans* was "in the forefront of Gertrude Stein's mind" because of attempts to get it published.[17] This would, of course, affect her style and, more important, cause a renewed interest in the problems of narrative. This is a plausible explanation for her decided lack of interest in playwriting at this time. But, as Wendy Steiner shows in her graphic "Chronology of Stein's Literary Genres," Stein continued to write portraits, descriptions, and essays in spite of her concentration on *The Making of Americans* and on narrative technique.[18]

I believe that the end of playwriting was the inevitable outcome of the kind of "program" Stein was pursuing in her first decade as a dramatist. The foregrounding of language in the theater is a difficult enterprise. As a writer with an idiosyncratic and privatized semiotic system, Stein would have had to face the public character of language in the theater. In the public forum of the theater, private meanings are lost; metatextual games played with written words are meaningless. One is left simply with sound—signifying nothing. Or with silence.

II

In the early twenties Stein wrote only a few plays like *A List* in which she successfully balanced written text and performance text: *Lend a Hand or Four Religions* (1922); *Capital Capitals* and *Jonas Julian Caesar and Samuel* (both in 1923). Other plays of this period foreshadow Stein's temporary withdrawal into theatrical silence. In *A Circular Play* (1920) and *Saints and Singing* (1922) the entire text is a written text—all side text, as it were. Stein records in these texts her ruminations about plays and playwriting (among other subjects). In *A Circular Play* the only concession Stein makes to the necessity that a play be a performable text is to suggest, from time to time, that a group (the eventual performers) gather in circles, dance in circles, play in circles, and sing in circles.[19] What they are to sing while they gather, dance, and play, she does not specify. In *Saints and Singing*, Stein describes the "origin of exhibiting acting":

Witnesses corroborate. I do not have to deny that the reason why I do not deny witnesses witnessing is because the origin the real origin of exhibiting acting is this. Mountains of saints singing. Mountains and mountains of saints singing and singing. Saints witnessing and corroborating. Mountains of saints witnessing and singing. Do sing please.[20]

She invites her saints to sing and her actors to act, but she does not provide the words for the performance. In both *A Circular Play* and *Saints and Singing*, the written text is the only text. The performance text is one which will be created by the performers. Naturally, a director can choose to divide the words of the script among the performers (as happened in the 1967 Carmines/Kornfeld production at the Judson Poets' Theater of *A Circular Play*, called *In Circles*), but the fact remains that Stein herself does not provide the performers with any words.

Another play of the early twenties, *A Village*, is a curious hybrid text which is similar to *A List* in its first few pages.[21] It opens with four villages (only numbered, not named), three of which speak in musical prose. But soon (four pages into the text) and quite abruptly, the villages disappear as speaking parts, never to resurface. The performance text is replaced by a narrative, or rather by a written text which purports to tell a story through "oratory" (an "oration of a history")—a story of a house, an accident, the furnishing of an estate, and of Amelia, a neighbor. It is as though this play is a record or an emblem of Stein's abandonment in 1923 of playwriting and her subsequent concentration on narrative.

Stein found her theatrical voice again in 1927 with *Four Saints in Three Acts*, an opera libretto she wrote at Virgil Thomson's suggestion. *Four Saints* reiterates but reverses the generic choice Stein made in *A Village*. Stein begins the play avowing her intention to write a narrative and ends by writing a play. In fact, Stein began the composition of *Four Saints* in the last notebook of a manuscript called "Regular regularly In narrative," a meditation on narrative which would eventually be included in *How to Write*. On the cover of notebook #6 of "Regular regularly," Stein writes, "end / Regular Regularly / VI / and beginning of Opera / Beginning of studies for an opera to be sung I."[22] Indeed, midway through this notebook she does begin *Four Saints*. Although she marks the separation between one manuscript and the next with a line drawn heavily and repeatedly across the page and though she announces "Beginning of Studies for an opera to be sung," she begins with what seems like a continuation of her meditation on narrative:

To know to know to love her so.
Four saints prepare for saints.
It makes it well fish.
. . . .
Four saints prepare for saints . . .
In narrative prepare for saints.
. . . .
A narrative of prepare for saints in narrative prepare for saints.
Remain to narrate to prepare two saints for saints.[23]

In effect Stein postpones the necessity of writing a play by proposing a narrative as a "preparation" for *Four Saints*. She then begins a narrative of "what happened today." Using the past tense, Stein tells of a trip to the country on a beautiful day and of a visit (presumably later in the day) from a "he," who "said he was hurrying" (12). The visitor's conversation is reported using the narrative convention of indirect discourse. The visitor's speech ends at the bottom of one notebook page of the manuscript, and Stein begins the next notebook page with a cautionary note: "This is how they do not like it." Since "they" do not like it, the format of the text changes from lengthy paragraphs, suitable to narrative, to a succession of single lines, and from a narrative of what happened today to an invitation to "Imagine four benches separately."[24] To "imagine four benches" is to move outside the text, but not back in time to a world of which the text is a report or a representation, but forward, to a world which the text is going to create—a movement from narrative to playwriting.

Shortly thereafter Stein urges herself to begin the play. "Begin three saints. Begin four saints" (12–13). But beginning is no easy task, and more narrative, more indirect discourse follow. Again Stein urges "Imagine imagine it imagine it in it" (14), but for a few more lines she holds to the idea of beginning *Four Saints* with a narrative:

> A narrative who do who does.
> A narrative to plan an opera.
> Four saints in three acts.
> A croquet scene and when they made their habits. (14)

The play ("Four Saints in Three Acts—A Croquet Scene") finally wins out, and Stein invokes Saint Therese, the principal character in the play.

Stein might not have returned to the writing of plays had Virgil Thomson not suggested that they collaborate on an opera. In his autobiography Thomson claims that Stein's "discovery of the opera as a poetic form" came through her friendship with him.[25] In fact, Stein had long been aware of opera as a poetic form.

As an undergraduate at Radcliffe, Stein had frequently attended the opera. In *The Autobiography of Alice B. Toklas*, Stein tells how her attendance at the opera interfered with her studying for her exam in William James's course:

Gertrude Stein had been going to the opera every night and going also to the opera in the afternoon and had been otherwise engrossed and it was the period of the final examinations, and there was the examination in William James' course. She sat down with the examination paper before her and she just could not. Dear Professor James, she wrote at the top of her paper. I am so sorry but really I do not feel a bit like an examination paper in philosophy to-day, and left.[26]

Although Stein claims that as an adult she had given up on music and the opera, she did attend a performance of Strauss's *Elektra* in London in 1913, about which she wrote to Mabel Dodge:

It made a deeper impression on me than anything since Tristan in my youth. He has done what Wagner tried to do and couldn't he has made real conversation. And he does it by intervals and relations directly without machinery. After all we are all modern.[27]

Stein's comments on Strauss, and particularly on the connection between *Elektra* and *Tristan*, demonstrate a sophisticated understanding
of the form and history of opera. Strauss was descended from Wagner: in his earliest works directly imitating his master; in *Salomé* and
Elektra exaggerating a Wagnerian tendency which Joseph Kerman
describes as the "idea of opera as symphonic poem."[28] Wagner in *Tristan* and Strauss in *Salomé* and *Elektra* were creating operas according
to the rules of symphonic organization. Both composers used the recurrence and variation of musical motifs to unify their compositions
in an organic whole which had less to do with the dramatic action, the
"machinery" characteristic of most opera, than with the musical patterns of non-operatic compositions. For Wagner, this was only a tendency never fully realized; for Strauss, the Wagnerian implication
was carried out (albeit without sustained distinction).

In 1913 when Stein saw *Elektra*, she was not contemplating a career as a librettist, but she was beginning to write plays, plays in which
she would shortly attempt to make her own "real conversations" without "machinery." The formal similarity of this work to her own writing did not escape her—"After all we are all modern."

In his history of the libretto, Patrick Smith traces the development of the modern libretto from Wagner through Edith Sitwell's
Façade to Jean Cocteau's *Oedipus Rex* and finally to Stein's *Four Saints*,
which took the "short step" from these predecessors to the "abstract
libretto." Smith sees *Tristan* as a sort of grandfather to *Four Saints*.

Wagner's infatuation with the musical side of the verse—that is, the variations
possible with the word-sounds—tended in its extreme compression to push
the words past the bounds of meaning into something bordering on pure
sound for its own sake. . . . The verse [Wagner's] thus takes on an abstract
quality responsive to its own inner world of assonance and alliteration as well
as, and perhaps more than, remaining a tool for understanding the story or
the characters. In this sense the verse foreshadows the "abstract poetry" fragmentation of Gertrude Stein in her librettos for Thomson, which derived
directly from Dada, but which, in libretto history, had, like Siegfried, another
unknown but powerful grandfather. *Tristan* is, of course, the opera in which
this abstract approach is most clearly revealed.[29]

While I am not convinced by the lineage Smith traces for Stein (see
the Epilogue), Stein was, indeed, familiar with all the predecessors
Smith mentions: with Wagner through his letters which she had read
and his operas which she had often heard; with Edith Sitwell whom
she met in Paris in 1925, two years after the controversial premiere
in London of Sitwell's opera *Façade* (music by William Walton); and
with Jean Cocteau whose Latin opera *Oedipus Rex* (composer, Stravin-
sky) used a narrator, was called an opera-oratorio (which is exactly

what Thomson called *Four Saints*), and was being written and performed while Stein was writing *Four Saints*. Thus, Stein would have become aware of opera as a poetic form even without Thomson's friendship.

Despite her familiarity with opera and her awareness of parallels between certain operas and her own plays, despite her designation of three of the texts in *Operas and Plays* as operas *(Four Saints in Three Acts, A Lyrical Opera Made by Two to Be Sung* [1928], and *Madame Recamier. An Opera* [1930]), and despite Thomson's commission of an opera libretto, I will be discussing *Four Saints* not as an opera, but as a play. In the first place, I see no textual characteristics to distinguish *Four Saints*, or either of the other two so-called operas, from the plays of this period. Moreover, Stein herself seems to have had trouble maintaining the generic distinction. The manuscript of *Madame Recamier* bears the subtitle, "An Opera,"[30] but when Stein mentions *Madame Recamier* in a 1930 letter to Henry McBride, she writes, "I have written a real play a poetic meditative conversational drama about Mme Recamier, I think even the small or big theatres might act it it is so like a real play . . . a really truly play."[31] In "Plays" she quotes from *Madame Recamier*, as one example of a "great number of plays"[32] and later in *Everybody's Autobiography*, she again calls it a play.[33] Similarly, she calls *Four Saints* an "opera,"[34] a "play,"[35] and a "drama."[36]

The nature of Stein's collaboration with Thomson is emblematic of her attitude toward opera as a formal imposition on her characteristic style. Writing about Neo-Romanticism, Thomson predicts a return to grand tragedy through the union of early modernism and Neo-Romanticism:

The first twenty years [of our century] occupied themselves with technic. The present age is concerned about feeling. [Only] when these elements [shall] have been . . . coordinated . . . [will there] be a way of living, of contemplating, and of writing grandiose tragedy.[37]

Apparently, Thomson saw his collaboration with Stein as the predicted coordination of the technical with the emotional, for he envisioned the product of that collaboration as a tragedy in imitation of eighteenth-century Italian opera, in spite of Stein's technical modernity. Thomson and Stein discussed the opera in January or February of 1927, and according to Thomson, they came to the following agreement as to its theme and form:

The theme we chose was of my suggesting; it was the working artist's working life, which is to say, the life we were both living. It was also my idea that good things comes in pairs. . . . This dualistic view made it possible, without going in for sex unduly, to have both male and female leads with second leads and choruses surrounding them. . . . I thought we should follow overtly, however, *the format of classical Italian opera*, which carries on the commerce of the play in dry recitative, extending the emotional moments into arias and set-pieces. And since the eighteenth-century *opera seria*, or basic Italian opera, required *a serious mythological subject with a tragic ending*, we agreed to follow that convention also.[38] (emphasis added)

From March to May 1927 Stein worked on the first two acts of the opera. Her letters to Thomson during this period suggest that the writing was not coming easily. In March she reports, "I think I have got St. Therese onto the stage, it has been an awful struggle and I think I can keep her on and gradually by the second act get St. Ignatius on and then they will both be on together but not at once in the third act."[39] In May she writes, "Life is too strenuous. I have not been able to write in a diary let alone a saint."[40]

Toward the end of May, then, she seems to have been unable to proceed, and in June she writes, "owing to a complication of things I have not gone further."[41] Nonetheless, she was able to show Thomson the first two acts before they both left Paris for the summer. Since Stein's numbering system is erratic (there are three first acts and one short second act which comes between two of the first acts), it is difficult to say exactly how much of the libretto she showed Thomson, but if she had gotten through Act 2 before June, she had probably completed almost half of it. Having seen this much of the opera, he must certainly have realized that she had not followed either "overtly" or covertly the "format of classical Italian opera" nor the "convention" of a "serious mythological subject with a tragic ending." *Four Saints* is not operatic by virtue of any intrinsic qualities. It is because Thomson set the play *Four Saints* to music that it became an opera. I would, in fact, suggest that the only "operas" Stein wrote were not those plays she called operas, but those that were eventually scored for voices as either operas or musicals: *Capital Capitals, Four Saints in Three Acts*, and *The Mother of Us All* (composer Virgil Thomson); *Doctor Faustus Lights the Lights, A Circular Play* (as *In Circles*), *Listen to Me*, and *A Manoir* (composer Al Carmines); *Ladies' Voices* (composer Vernon Martin); *Look and Long* (composers Florence Wickham and Marvin Schwartz); *In a Garden* (composer Meyer Kupferman); *Three Sisters Who Are Not Sisters* (composer Ned Rorem); and *Photograph* (composer Marvin Kalmanoff).

Although Thomson did not introduce Stein to "opera as a poetic form," he did have an impact on the direction her writing was to take. Thomson had long been an admirer of Stein's work. He writes in his autobiography that his introduction to *Tender Buttons* while a student at Harvard "changed [his] life"[42] and that he was "addicted from Harvard days to *Tender Buttons* and to *Geography and Plays*."[43] He even tried setting some of *Tender Buttons* to music, apparently without success (the compositions have not survived even as juvenilia).

Thomson not only admired Stein's work, but he was also in a position to be useful to her. He was well-connected both in France and in the United States and had powerful and generous patrons. Thomson was assiduous in his efforts to bring Stein's writing to public attention, especially when it was connected to his own work: Stein's words accompanied by his music. With Madame Louise Langlois, a French salonist and his good friend, he translated into French "Water Pipe" (1916) and "A Saint in Seven" (1922); with Georges Hugnet, "Dix Portraits" (which was published by Hugnet, who had met Stein through Thomson) and parts of *The Making of Americans*. More important, Thomson set a number of Stein's texts to music before he ever suggested that they collaborate on *Four Saints*.

Just after his first meeting with Stein (in February or March 1926), Thomson set "Susie Asado" (a 1913 portrait) to music. Stein knew nothing of this until Thomson brought her the score on New Year's Day 1927. He followed this presentation, in February of the same year, with the composition of the music for "Preciosilla" (also a 1913 portrait) and in April with *Capital Capitals*. Thomson performed his settings of Stein's texts at the houses of literary salonists, Natalie Barney and the Duchesse de Clermont-Tonnerre. In Thomson's words, "all that winter and spring . . . I was serving Gertrude Stein as translator, impresario, music setter, and literary agent."[44]

When Stein saw Thomson's score of "Susie Asado," she expressed in a note to Thomson her eagerness to hear the piece performed: "I like its looks immensely and want to frame it and Miss Toklas who knows more than looks says the things in it please her a lot and when can I know a little other than its looks."[45] I have no evidence of the date of Stein's aural introduction to "Susie," but since she and Thomson began seeing each other regularly after her receipt on New Year's Day of the score (Thomson even performing Satie's *Socrate* in its entirety, and privately, for Stein and Toklas in his quarters in Paris), it is likely that Thomson quickly gratified Stein's wish to hear the piece. In any case, she would have heard it performed publicly (along with "Preciosilla") by Thomson at an after-tea program at the home of Natalie Barney in February 1927.

About the experience of hearing her words set to music Stein writes in *The Autobiography of Alice B. Toklas* that "she [Stein] delighted in listening to her words framed by his [Thomson's] music."[46] In *Everybody's Autobiography* she explains why: "Each time a musician does something with the words it makes it do what they never did do."[47] It was what she could learn about her own writing when it was accompanied by music that made her association with Thomson an effective force in her development. The lessons began before the composition of *Four Saints*.

One of Thomson's special interests was English musical declamation. He was sensitive to the musical rhythms of speech, possibly because of his early choir and glee club training. In *The Musical Scene* he writes about the connection between music and language:

Way back in the mind, where music gets born, it has a closer concordance with language and with gesture than it can ever possibly have with the obscure movements of the viscera or with states of the soul.[48]

In Gertrude Stein, Thomson saw a writer who was as aware as he of the affinities between music and language, and whose writing was, as Thomson describes it, with particular reference to *Capital Capitals*, "closer to musical timings than to speech timings."[49] Thomson explains his intentions in setting Stein to music as follows:

My hope in putting Gertrude Stein to music had been to break, crack open, and solve for all time anything still waiting to be solved, which was almost everything, about English musical declamation. My theory was that if a text is set correctly for the sound of it, the meaning will take care of itself. And the Stein texts, for prosodizing in this way, were manna. With meanings already abstracted, or absent, or so multiplied that choice among them was impossible, there was no temptation toward tonal illustration. . . . You could make a setting for sound and syntax only, then add, if needed, an accompaniment equally functional.[50]

This is exactly what Thomson accomplished with "Susie Asado." The music complements the words, the musical declamation closely following Stein's language—its "sound and syntax." The piano accompaniment matches the simplicity of Stein's vocabulary and the discontinuity of her syntax. What Stein would have heard in "Susie" was the articulation of the music inherent in her writing. She would also have heard that the music does not overpower the words, that the words lead and the music follows, an undoubtedly reassuring arrangement.

In "Preciosilla" Thomson tried a different tactic. The music is not complement, but contrast to the text. For Stein's text, Thomson devised a formal musical arrangement (an old-fashioned one at that), dividing it into recitative and aria. John Cage describes the effect of this juxtaposition of music to words thus: "The words remind us that we are living in the twentieth century; the music convinces us that we are listening to a baroque cantata."[51]

Capital Capitals was the last Stein text which Thomson set to music before composing *Four Saints*. It is a play, in style quite similar to *A List*; it too has a written text with wordplay apparent only to a reader; it too has a performance text organized musically on the basis of word sounds rather than word meanings. The concept around which Stein's words revolve in *Capital Capitals* is the rather simple one that "capital" is a homonym with multiple meanings which Stein sets forth in the first few lines and repeats at intervals throughout the play:

  1) n. an upper-case letter
"Capitally be.
Capitally see."
  2) adj. excellent
"Capital very good."
  3) n. a stock of accumulated goods
"Capital. He has capital."
  4) n. the city in which the seat of government is located
"A state has a capital a country has a capital."[52]

There are four speaking parts in the play, called "First Capital, Second Capital," and so on. Thomson scored the work for four male voices with intermittent piano accompaniment. The interconnectedness of Stein's phrases through rhyme, assonance, consonance, alliteration, and modulated repetition, which I described earlier in my discussion of *A List*, is present also in *Capital Capitals*. Thomson's scansion draws our attention to the word-music of the text by stressing the sound-linked and repeated words and, sometimes, by breaking rhythmic stride at such words. However, Thomson also emphasizes the essentially static nature of Stein's text. It is as though he were determined to show that, in spite of the music in the words, there is no music in the prose lines. *Capital Capitals* is set entirely in recitative. At no point is the text allowed to expand lyrically. The longer passages are not arias but, as John Cage calls them, "chants." Cage also points out that "in one instance, seventy-one words of text roll by on one tone, though out of the total of fifty-five such chant-like passages in this song, the average number of words appearing on a repeated tone without any given rhythmic pattern is a more modest seventeen and a half."[53]

The effect of such notationally uniform recitative is to point to the monotonous or hypnotic quality of the language. At the same time, the rhythms of the musical declamation create a kind of urgency, a pressure on the words through speed and through an intensification at the end of passages, which leads us to expect a climax which the words never provide and which the music only prepares for, but also never provides.

Thomson uses the piano for the same effect. To the piano goes the lyric burden of the piece. The piano reminds us fleetingly of tunes the names of which we cannot recall. It imitates drum rolls and trumpet flourishes, and provides, in its own voice, trembling, melodramatic, preparatory flurries. In other words, the piano, even more than the recitative, prepares us for climaxes that are not to be experienced.

As a spoken text, *Capital Capitals* might seem sensually and rhythmically compelling, but when accompanied by music, another of its qualities becomes prominent. It becomes clear that the rhythms of Stein's prose are not progressive, but circular, verging on static. There is no crescendo in Stein's verbal music. The words go on, but they go nowhere: first, because they are always doubling back on themselves through repetition, and second, because there is in Stein's prose no hierarchy of emphasis.

Whether Thomson arranged his music as a reflection of Stein's text or in opposition to it, his belief in the affinity between music and language was tempered by his sense of the limitations of both media, which keep them from achieving identity and which mean that music has something to contribute to language and language to music in any vocal composition. In discussing *Four Saints*, Thomson addresses the differences between the two:

What gave this work [*Four Saints*] so special a vitality? The origin of that lay in its words, of course, the music having been created in their image. Music, however, contains an energy long since lost to language, an excitement created by the contest of two rhythmic patterns, one of lengths and one of stresses. A pattern made up of lengths alone is static, and the stuttering of mere stresses is hypnotic. But together, and contrasted, they create tension and release; and this is the energy that makes music sail, take flight, get off the ground. By applying it to the text of Gertrude Stein, I had produced a pacing that is implied in that text, if you wish, but that could never be produced without measured extensions. Speech alone lacks music's forward thrust.[54]

Thomson associates music with directional movement—"forward thrust," "sail," "take flight," "get off the ground"—and language with a vitality that is more stationary, either "static" or "hypnotic."

Although spoken language and music both produce sounds through a system of written signs and both move forward through

time, language is usually less forcefully progressive than music because words have a referential dimension through which language
glances out as it moves forward. Stein's prose seems close to music
exactly because its words are nonreferential and because it is organized around sound rather than sense. That was the source of their
appeal to Thomson. However, Thomson demonstrates in his scoring
that even Stein's musical prose lacks the energy and direction of music. Granted this idea of energy and forward thrust pertains to the
kind of music Thomson wrote and envisioned writing. There is music, like jazz, in which the forward movement coexists with and is
equivalent to the circular movement of passages which are tangential
to the forward line, passages which improvise and elaborate on suggestions implicit in the melody. Stein's writing is analogous to this
kind of music. However, Thomson's musical accompaniment of Stein
is almost always in opposition to this tangential and circular quality of
her prose. By this contrast, the immobility of Stein's prose is heightened.

When Thomson commissioned *Four Saints* he was, in effect, forc-
ing Stein to write once again for the theater. At the same time, he was
composing music for and performing Stein's texts; thus, she could
hear for the first time her words in performance. This experience
would have called her attention to the way her words "played" in
time. Face-to-face with the dynamism of performance, Stein had a
new metadramatic theme to explore.

After some hesitation Stein settled down in *Four Saints* to write a
play whose language and structure oppose the dynamic thrust of performance, a play that emphasizes the static qualities of language and
of the written text. The text initiates a performance; it provides the
songs for singing, the words for speaking. It sketches out action and
the spaces in which the action can take place. At the same time, it
counteracts the very performance it initiates in a kind of counter-text,
a written text which asserts itself at every moment of performance, a
counter-text that proceeds at a slower pace than the performed text.

This bifurcation of the text was noticed by almost all the review-
ers of the original 1934 production and the 1952 revival. When discussing the Stein libretto independent of its musical score, critics
found it at once musically and sensually enjoyable *and* conceptually
perplexing. It seemed, at the same time, to suit, even to inspire,
Thomson's score *and* to be opposed to it. Kenneth Burke noted a
"private planfulness . . . a deliberation which too often makes her
[Stein's] lines elusive," but at the same time, found that this deliberate
"nonsense [of Stein's] has established its great musicality. Even as
nonsense it sings well."[55] Stark Young, writing for the *New Republic*,

saw the duality of the text as based, on the one hand, on its "unbroken air of spontaneity, its charming and capricious flights" and, on the other, on the "hidden unity of the whole."[56] Edith Isaacs, in *Theatre Arts Monthly*, praised the choreography, the music, and the direction but found the words "only *partially* successful. . . . [They] evoked in the collaborating artists the working ideas for the delightful scheme." But Isaacs criticized the text on the grounds that it was "dully repetitive . . . often ugly and unsingable" (emphasis added).[57] Gilbert Seldes remarked on the contrasting moods in Stein's libretto. "Unlike most words for opera, they carry, from time to time, a charge of emotion, and the great difficulty of Miss Stein's method is that she interferes with the very emotion she creates."[58]

In reviewing the 1952 production, Brooks Atkinson saw a contrast between the "form and style" of the libretto, which he found "admirable," and "the content" and "emotional values," which he found "unsatisfying," "full of a feeling of aimlessness," "repetitious," and "desultory."[59] Reviewing the same production in the *New York Journal American*, Miles Kastendieck described Stein's libretto as both "a state of mind" and an "experience in sound."[60] Despite the fact that some of these critics were unsympathetic to Stein and to avantgarde theater art in general, they do articulate the response that an audience might have had to the opposition between the written text and the performance text, an opposition created by Stein.

To counteract the momentum of performance requires a heroic effort on the part of the dramatist. In the theater the forward march of time is inexorable. Speech and action (and in the case of opera, music) have a "kinetic thrust," as Calderwood puts it, that cannot be ignored.[61] This thrust through time is the essential feature of performance. Colin Cherry writes that "speech is bound to the time continuum; we must receive it as it comes, instant by instant . . . it is a continuous stream."[62] Michael Kirby says essentially the same thing about action and about the structure of performance.

Action contains (is) an energy that flows through time for a particular period. It is by its very nature perceptually or mentally dynamic. It creates expectancy or anticipation of that which has not yet happened. . . . The energy or force flowing through the present moment moves toward the future. This dynamic energy may be called the "momentum" of an action.[63]

The structure of a performance exists primarily in time. Time, the major dimension of performance, can be seen as a sequence of present moments, each of which moves away to become part of the past. This movement is unidirectional. The parts of the continuum have a fixed order and are not interchangeable. . . . We cannot "reread" a moment in performance. We cannot cut out intervening experience and place a past moment alongside a present one for direct comparison.[64]

Speech and action, which constitute the performance, are dynamic, and they move along a continuum. But the performance takes place in a space and is a visual as well as a temporal phenomenon. The flow of speech and action is checked, as it were, by the way the eye perceives the performance in space—instant by instant. Really then, the dynamism of performance, while it is continuous, is more like a succession of present instants than a seamless flow. It is at once continuous and discontinuous.

The actor, the set, and the text can either increase continuity or decrease it. Usually the text will provide informational connections across time. The bits of information will cohere and their coherence will provide a kind of continuity. The use of the same set from one scene to another will also provide continuity. The actor is perhaps the source of greatest continuity in a performance. He is *in propria persona* always present and always the same. He occupies space and he continues. He is present to the eye in each separate moment of performance, but he is also the conduit of speech and action on their journey forward through time.

In *Four Saints* Stein emphasizes the discontinuity of performance rather than its continuity. Her language is static and her syntax is fractured. The structure of the written text seems to militate against the actor in his role as conduit of the current of performance. If, as Elizabeth Burns writes, the actor is "an interloper [who] intervenes between the playwright and the audience,"[65] then Stein is a playwright who is trying to minimize the intervention of the actor, to oppose his dynamism and, in a sense, to prevent him from acting. What Stein tries to attain in *Four Saints* is a direct contact with her audience, without intermediary. In other words, she tries to write the actor out of *Four Saints* and to write the writer into it.

III

Virgil Thomson has suggested that *Four Saints* is about "the working artist's life" as symbolized by the saints. I would say, rather, that *Four Saints* is about the artist at work; the artist is Gertrude Stein and her work is the writing of the play, *Four Saints*. Stein, the writer, is actually a character in her own play. As Richard Bridgman has noted, "almost two-thirds of the text is composed of authorial statement and commentary."[66] Thomson obscured this fact in production by parceling out the authorial commentary to two figures (called "commere" and "compere"), both of whom seem in performance to be stage directors. Even at that, however, they discuss not so much the performance of the play—the stage business—as they do the composition—the business of writing. Thomson divided Gertrude Stein, but he did not conquer her. Notwithstanding Thomson's alteration of the text, the writer of the play makes her presence felt during performance.

At the beginning of the play Stein maintains a running commentary on the writing process (and progress): self-criticism, self-encouragement, progress reports, plans and preparations for writing, and discussions of the difficulty or ease of writing. She even includes dates to mark the course of her composition: April 1, Easter. The process of composition is as palpable as the procession of Saints in Act 3.

Once the play gets well under way, once Saint Ignatius and Saint Therese begin to speak, Stein does not so much discuss the text that is being written or urge herself to write more of it, as deal with the written text as a plan for performance. However, it is a plan which is never settled because we are meant to see the writing and the performance as simultaneous acts.

There are a Saint Plan and a Saint Settlement among the cast of characters, and the necessity of planning and settling is brought up at intervals throughout the play, most often when Stein or her saints are having difficulty in deciding how the plan is to be settled. The famous question/refrain—"How many saints are there in it?"—is one of many similar questions: "How many acts are there in it?" "How many nails are there in it?" "How many floors are there in it?" "How many doors?" "How many windows?" and "How much of it is finished?" "It is easy to measure a settlement," says Saint Therese (30). But it is not easy to measure this play because it is never settled.

The question of how many saints are in the play has several answers, all of which skirt the issue:

Saint Therese. How many saints are there in it.
Saint Therese. There are very many many saints in it.
Saint Therese. There are as many saints as there are in it.
Saint Therese. How many saints are there in it.
Saint Therese. There are there are there are saints saints in it.
[Stein then names seven saints, hardly a complete list.]
Saint Therese. How many saints are there in it.
Saint Cecilia. How many saints are there in it.
Saint Therese. There are as many saints as there are in it.
Saint Cecilia. There are as many saints as there are saints in it. (28)

In the second-to-the-last scene (in which Saint Settlement and Saint Anne say that "there can be two Saint Annes if you like"), Stein writes:

> They have to be.
> They have to be.
> They have to be to see.
> To see to say.
> Laterally they may. (47)

If we see saints, they exist. Accordingly, in the last scene, Stein specifies that the saints ("All Saints") be lined laterally to the left and right of Saint Ignatius for our perusal. As the play ends, we can count the saints and answer one of the questions posed in the text.

As for the number of acts, the title promises us three, but the title, written first, cannot possibly measure the play, which has not yet been written. In fact, the play has four named acts, but there are three first acts, two second acts, two third acts, and one fourth act, making a total of eight acts. The only certainty regarding the number of acts in the play is that which is obvious at the end: "Last Act. / Which is a fact." No matter how many acts there are in it, the play is certain to finish. It is only when the play is finished that we will know how many acts there were in it, just as the number of doors, windows, floors, and nails in a house cannot be ascertained until the building is complete, for even the most carefully laid plans can be changed.

Four Saints is certainly pre-planned. The written text exists, and it is the plan that the performance follows. However, we are made to feel that the plan is being created in our presence, as the performance proceeds. Stein writes the play so that during performance she will seem to be feeding the actors their lines. So, for example, Stein will make a statement, "Who settles a private life," which is then supposed to be echoed by an actor—"Saint Therese. Who settles a private life." This pattern recurs as in: "None to be behind. Enclosure. / Saint Therese. None to be behind. Enclosure" (20); and "To be interested in Saint Therese fortunately. / Saint Therese. To be interested in Saint Therese fortunately" (25); and "Nobody visits more than they do visits them. / Saint Therese. Nobody visits more than they do visits them Saint Therese" (16).

In the last example Saint Therese behaves like the ventriloquist's dummy, who, when instructed, "Say hello, Charlie," says "Hello Charlie." Saint Therese echoes her own name and forces us to accept Stein's instructions, the side text, as part of the performance text. The imposition of the written text on the performance text occurs also with the act/scene divisions of *Four Saints*. It is sometimes accomplished by rhyming a line of spoken text with the scene number, as in:

Scene X

When. (31)

or by a syntactical connection of the written text to the performance text, as in:

Scene VI

With Seven.

Scene VII

With eight.

Scene VIII (42)

Or by a homophonic connection, such as:

Scene One

And seen one. Very likely. (35)

At one point, Stein makes the scenes themselves speakers and makes their speeches rhyme with their names:

Scene eight. To Wait.
Scene one. And. begun.
Scene two. To and to.
Scene three. Happily be.
Scene Four. Attached or.
Scene Five. Sent to derive.
Scene Six. Let it mix.
Scene Seven. Attached eleven.
Scene Eight. To wait.   (29)

In all of these examples, an enactor could choose to ignore the connection Stein makes between written notation and spoken text, but the connection is there nonetheless.

Often Stein does not give the enactor a choice. The act/scene announcement is made twice, once in writing and once (sometimes more than once) in performance. For example:

Act One

Saint Therese. Preparing in as you might say.
Saint Therese was pleasing. In as you might say.

Saint Therese Act One.
Saint Therese has begun to be in act one.
Saint Therese and begun.
Saint Therese as sung.
Saint Therese act one.
Saint Therese and begun.
Saint Therese and sing and sung.
Saint Therese in an act one. Saint Therese questions. (23)

And:

Scene V
Many many saints can be left to many many saints scene five left to many many saints. (26)

And:

Scene VII
One two three four five six seven scene seven.
Saint Therese scene seven.
Saint Therese scene scene seven. (27)

And:

Scene II
Would it do if there was a Scene II. (24)

In the last example Stein discusses only the possibility of having a Scene 2. "Would it do?" *Four Saints* abounds in the use of conditionals, adding to the sense of uncertainty and tentativeness in the play. If a Scene 2 would not do, would Stein eliminate it? As might be expected, uncertainty is most intense in the first half of the play. As the play takes shape it leaves fewer questions unanswered. But in Act 1, almost nothing has been determined. After a five-page discussion of how Saint Therese and Saint Ignatius are to appear (whether sitting or standing, moving or still, on the stage or off), Stein has this to say:

Saint Ignatius could be in porcelain actually.
Saint Ignatius could be in porcelain actually while he was young and standing.
Saint Therese could not be young and standing she could be sitting.

Saint Ignatius could be in porcelain actually actually in porcelain standing.

Saint Therese could be admittedly could be in moving seating. Saint Therese could be in moving sitting.

Saint Therese could be.

Saint Ignatius could be.

Saint Ignatius could be in porcelain actually in porcelain standing. (20)

The prolonged discussion of the disposition of the actors on the stage (which the text does not resolve, but which must of course be resolved in performance) proceeds through a series of contradictory directions. At the beginning of her deliberations, Stein repeats four times that Saint Therese is seated, but following the fourth announcement, Stein immediately contradicts herself: "Saint Therese not seated." This direction is repeated, and then, as if to reconcile the two statements, Stein adds "Saint Therese not seated at once" (16). Presumably, Saint Therese is to begin by standing and is then to sit. "Saint Therese once seated. There are a great many places and persons near together. Saint Therese seated and not surrounded" (16). Once seated, Saint Therese will be isolated from the other performers. The contradiction seems to be resolved. But another apparently insoluble stage direction is introduced. Saint Therese is to be "very nearly half inside and half outside outside the house." Stein specifies that "the garden" too is "outside and inside of the wall." While a garden can quite easily be split in two, a person cannot be so divided. So Saint Therese is neither in nor out, but somewhere in between. Poised on a threshold, she is, as Stein says, "About to be" (16). Then Stein introduces Saint Ignatius, who, she tells us, "could be" and finally "is standing." The positions of the two principal saints seem settled, until Stein launches into a passage which epitomizes the text in process:

Saint Therese seated and not standing half and half of it and not half and half of it seated and not standing surrounded and not seated and not seated and not standing and not surrounded and not surrounded and not not not seated not seated not seated not surrounded not seated and Saint Ignatius standing standing not seated Saint Therese not standing not standing and Saint Ignatius not standing standing surrounded as if in once yesterday. In place of situations. Saint Therese could be very much interested not only in settlement Saint Settlement and this not with with this wither wither they must be additional. Saint Therese having not commenced. (17)

Saint Therese, who was about to be, has not yet commenced because the question of whether she is to sit or stand has not yet been decided.

Because of contradictory directions and conditional suggestions, the writing of the play seems always to be in process. Composition becomes a performance event. The writing of the play appears to be going on before our eyes. At the same time, the unfinished quality of the written text, its very eventfulness, immobilizes the actors and the performance text. Like Saint Therese, who is half in and half out, the performance itself is suspended in a kind of limbo. It consists entirely of preparation, beginning with the narrative which prepares for the play, followed by a play which prepares for a performance, and ending with the only fact, which is the last act.

Even Stein's inspiration for Saint Therese and Saint Ignatius is immobile. Stein explained that she had imagined Saint Therese as being like the photographs she saw in a store window, of a girl becoming a nun—still shots, one following another, the immobilization of a process by dividing it into the frozen moments of its unfolding.[67] Stein refers to this image of Therese's saintly development within the play:

> Saint Therese could be photographed having been dressed like a lady and then they taking out her head changed it to a nun and a nun a saint and a saint so. (17)

As for Saint Ignatius, he too has been transfixed by Stein's suggestion that he be a porcelain statue, which she later explained referred to an actual figurine, again in a store window, which she imagined to be Saint Ignatius.[68]

Saint Therese, the photograph, and Saint Ignatius, the statue, are represented in a play where even the syntax of the sentences tends toward a kind of suspended animation. The arias for which this opera is famous ("Pigeons on the grass alas," "When this you see remember me," and "wed dead said led") occur in the last quarter of the play. For the most part the play lurches past us with stuttering, choppy, and flat prose. Stein pares her vocabulary to the most ordinary of monosyllables: as, it, be, at, in, not, the, is, an, was, would, out, might, could, if, with, how, they, this, that, hurt, found, like, and make, for example. Most of these words are normally unstressed, and all are too short to be mellifluous.

Repetition, which in *A List* had knit phrases simultaneously to preceding and subsequent phrases, producing a fabric of words united by similarities but always changing through modulation, becomes in *Four Saints* an annoying case of stuttering. The text becomes stalled on phrases, sometimes only for a moment, "he said he said feeling very nearly everything as it had been as if he could be precious be precious to like like it as it had been" (12), sometimes longer:

Who settles a private life.
Saint Therese. Who settles a private life.
Saint Therese. Who settles a private life.
Saint Therese. Who settles a private life.
Saint Therese. Who settles a private life. (16–17)

At one point the phrase "Once in a while" is repeated twenty-six times in succession (30). Many of the sentences in *Four Saints* remind us of a record which has caught the phonograph needle in one groove, or they seem like a kind of mirror writing where the words which come into the text are immediately reflected in reverse order:

Saint Ignatius. Withdrew with with withdrew. . . .
Saint Ignatius. Occurred withdrew.
Saint Ignatius. Withdrew Occurred. (33)

Some sentences pivot around a center, the words held in place by a kind of centrifugal force of syntax: "Saints all in all Saints" (29). Many passages come to us in stages, like revised compositions where the variations are never erased:

He asked for a distant magpie as if they made a difference.
He asked for a distant magpie as if he asked for a distant magpie as if that made a difference.
He asked as if that made a difference.
He asked for a distant magpie.
He asked for a distant magpie.
As if that made a difference he asked for a distant magpie as if that made a difference. He asked as if that made a difference. A distant magpie. He asked for a distant magpie. He asked for a distant magpie. (37)

Within her stalled sentences Stein minimizes or manipulates grammatical indicators of activity. Verbs are often eliminated and sentences replaced by noun phrases, like the familiar "pigeons on the grass" or like the following:

Saint Therese in a cart drawn by oxen moving around. . . .
Saint Therese in time. (24)

And:

> Saint Ignatius and more.
> Saint Ignatius with as well. . . .
> Saint Ignatius finally. . . .
> Saint Ignatius with it just. . . .
> Saint Ignatius with it Tuesday. (25)

The preferred verb form is the participle, most often used as a verbal, as in:

> Saint Therese unsurrounded by reason of it being so cold that they stayed away. (24)

> Saint Ignatius well bound. (25)

> Saint Settlement aroused by the recall of Amsterdam. (29)

The effect of the verbal is to immobilize the subject, the passive recipient of the action, the inactive center of movement. At one point Stein asks, "What is the difference between a picture and pictured" (21). The difference is that the former is a noun and the latter a participial adjective, and further that one refers to form and the other to content. But both words (noun and verbal) focus on the immobilized object (the picture) rather than the activity (picture-making). Even when the participle indicates that the subject is the actor, not the receiver, it avoids placing the activity in time, as in the following examples:

> Saint Therese seated. (17)

> Saint Ignatius standing. (17)

> Saint Therese advancing. (19)

> Saint Therese using a cart with oxen to go about and as well as if she were there. (24)

The participle pictures the subject in a steady state. Activity, in these examples, has neither beginning nor end. By using verbs as adjectives, Stein forces the performance into a series of tableaux, in which action is transformed into a quality, with no reference to time.

When Stein does refer to time in the play, it is to render it a meaningless measurement. For instance, memory, which is normally a present evocation of a past event or entity, is used in the following passage with an apparent disregard for its temporal function:

It is very easy in winter to remember winter spring and summer it
is very easy in winter to remember spring and winter and summer
it is very easy in winter to remember summer spring and winter it
is very easy in winter to remember spring and summer and winter.
(13)

It is possible in one winter to remember a winter gone by or to com-
pare the current season to a generalized memory of past winters, but
as the passage stands, it states that one remembers "winter in winter."
One cannot remember something one is "in." Since one must be out
of and past winter in order to remember it, the passage causes temporal confusion.

The following passage presents a temporal impossibility:

In the morning to be changed from the morning to the morning
in the morning. A scene of changing from the morning to the
morning. (25)

Change, like memory, is a function of time. To change is to move
from one form or identity to another, from the past (before the
change) to a different time (after the change). Change cannot occur
without the passage of time. Therefore, there cannot be a change
from the morning to the morning. If time does not change, then
nothing can change.

A similar confusion is created by the following statements:

It is no doubt not at all the following morning that it is very much
later very much earlier. (29)

It is to-morrow on arriving at a place to pass before the last. (29)

Commencing again yesterday. (33)

These instances of temporal confusion are only reflections in minia-
ture of the larger time warp created by the play itself.

I have said that in *Four Saints* Stein makes the writing process a
part of the performance. In doing this, she blurs the temporal distinction between writing, planning, and performance. Stein conflates
the time of planning (past), the time of writing (past), the time of
rehearsal (past), and the time of performance (present). She also syn-
chronizes these activities so that they occur at the same rate of speed.
Because the sensual stimuli of performance (music, action, and
speech) move at a faster tempo than the conceptualizing activities
(planning and writing), Stein immobilizes the former in order to ac-

commodate the latter. We feel that all of these activities occur simultaneously in a very slow-moving present.

The Thomson/Grosser arrangement of the text obscured its purpose and meaning by disguising the authorial voice and by ignoring the improvisational illusion that Stein created. Instead, the production of *Four Saints* emphasized the sensuality and musicality of the text. Of course, the play does have its musical side. As I have already noted, Stein provides a performance text and writes some arias. But Stein never relinquishes her hold on the text, never withdraws, as the playwright usually does. "When this you see," she writes, "Remember me" (47). Even when the written text is allowed to become a song, Stein, the poet, is its singer. We must not ignore the fact that the arias in this opera are passages of unassigned text. Even "Pigeons on the Grass" is a Stein song, although Thomson had Saint Ignatius sing it. This is how the aria appears in the original text:

Scene II

Pigeons on the grass alas.
Pigeons on the grass alas.
Short longer grass short longer longer shorter yellow grass Pigeons large pigeons on the shorter longer yellow grass alas pigeons on the grass.
If they were not pigeons what were they.
If they were not pigeons on the grass alas what were they. He had heard of a third and he asked about it it was a magpie in the sky. If a magpie in the sky on the sky can not cry if the pigeon on the grass alas can alas and to pass the pigeon on the grass alas and the magpie in the sky on the sky and to try and to try alas on the grass alas the pigeon on the grass the pigeon on the grass and alas. They might be very well very well very well they might be they might be very well they might be very well very well they might be. (36)

In an interview, Stein explained the genesis of this aria:

I was walking in the gardens of the Luxembourg in Paris. It was the end of summer the grass was yellow. I was sorry that it was the end of summer and I saw the big fat pigeons in the yellow grass and I said to myself, pigeons on the yellow grass, alas, and I kept on writing pigeons on the grass, alas, short longer grass, short longer longer shorter yellow grass pigeons large pigeons on the shorter longer yellow grass, alas pigeons on the grass, and I kept on writing until I had emptied myself of the emotion.[69]

By incorporating the moment of creation and the improvised product of that moment into the work to be performed, Stein once again violates the temporal boundaries between the creation of the written text and its performance.[70]

IV

In *A List* words are objects in a composition. The text is a product, something to occupy space in a book and in a theater. In *Four Saints*, words are events in the composition of a play text; the text is a process, something occurring in time.

The representation of the process of composing in the composition violates the most basic dramatic convention: that a play is a fictive utterance that is "detached" from the circumstances and conditions of its creation. A play pretends to be a series of natural utterances, the verbal acts of real persons on particular occasions in response to a particular set of circumstances, but unlike the natural utterances it imitates, the play does not occupy a specific and unique point in time and space; it is not historically unique. It is not an event, but an artifact, and because it is an artifact, the utterances it imitates can recur.

In violating this convention by making *Four Saints* represent the historically unique event of its creation, Stein shows that, in fact, the only process of which a play can be the natural utterance is the process of composition, that all other mimeses are false representations. Of course, once Stein's words are committed to paper, process of necessity becomes product. If the product is a play, its enactment again and again, its recurrence, is guaranteed. Its detachment from the creator and the circumstances of its creation is assured. Stein's mimesis is as much of an illusion as any other. To sustain this illusion Stein makes her play like a landscape, a space in which time stands still. In this landscape she preserves the historically unique moment of composition.

To the doubting, those who would insist that time cannot stand still in a play and does not in *Four Saints*, Stein offers the following parable:

Magpies are in the landscape that is they are in the sky of a landscape, they are black and white. . . . When they are in the sky they do something that I have never seen any other bird do they hold themselves up and down and look flat against the sky.

A very famous French inventor of things that have to do with stabilisation in aviation told me that what I told him magpies did could not be done by any bird but anyway whether the magpies at Avila do do it or do not at least they look as if they do do it. They look exactly like the birds in the Annunciation pictures the bird which is the Holy Ghost and rests flat against the side sky very high.[71]

Despite the doubts of the expert, the hapless French inventor who serves as her foil, Stein maintains that moving birds stand still against the sky. Impossible? Perhaps, but then Stein insists only that the birds seem stationary. Stein perceives them so because she has seen paintings in which such birds are indeed inanimate and therefore can rest flat against the sky. It is not too fanciful to see Stein's feat in *Four Saints* as comparable to the immobilization of the magpie in the paintings of the Annunciation. Through her "black and white" birds, the words of her text, she conveys an impression of stasis convincing enough to affect our perception of her play in performance. When the written words exist as perceptible and energetic language (live birds), they still appear motionless, as do the stage activities they instigate. In this illusionary landscape, where words make time stand still, we can see Gertrude Stein, the playwright, at work.

V

The new beginning in playwriting which Stein made in 1927 with *Four Saints* was not immediately productive. She wrote only three plays in 1928 and one in 1929. In summer 1927, while working on *Four Saints*, Stein had begun the novel *Lucy Church Amiably*, the composition of which was to extend well into 1929. During 1928 and 1929, Stein was also preoccupied with the acquisition of her country house at Bilignin. She and Alice finally moved into the house in spring 1929 after prolonged and complicated maneuvers to obtain the title to the property. Moreover, between 1927 and 1929 Stein composed five of the eight essays which make up *How to Write* (published in 1931), accounting for 338 of the book's 395 pages. Stein's concentration on these projects explains perhaps not only the lull in playwriting but also the overall scarcity of short works composed in any genre during these years.

Although Stein wrote few plays from 1927 to 1929, she continued in *How to Write* to explore the twin themes of language in space and language in time, the same themes that had surfaced in *A List*, *Four Saints*, and other early lang-scape plays. In *How to Write*, however, Stein was concerned not with language in the theater but with language in books, not with performance but with writing. In *How to Write* she opposes, not the dynamism of performance, but the dynamism of language itself, its linearity and continuity. How to hold each

word still, like the painted birds of the Annunciation, how to prevent
the connection of one word to another and how to halt the forward-
moving flight of sentences were matters Stein tried to resolve in *How
to Write*.

In *How to Write*, Stein discusses three components of writing: vocabulary, sentences, and paragraphs. For Stein the most "agreeable"
sentences are "successions of words"[72] in which "every word is at one
time" (142). What Stein means by "succession" is not continuity but
contiguity. One word lies next to the other, but there are no logical
or grammatical connections between words.

Through most of *How to Write* Stein questions the necessity of
grammar in the creation of sentences. "The question is if you have a
vocabulary have you any need of grammar except for explanation
that is the question, communication and direction repetition and intuition that is the question" (60). Obviously we do need grammar if
we are to communicate and to explain. The sentence is "very hard to
save" (30) from the tyranny of grammar, precisely because "it is impossible to avoid meaning and if there is meaning and it says what it
does there is grammar" (71).

In Stein's opinion, however, to accept grammar is to sacrifice that
"agreeable" succession of words in which each component is given
equal value. There are "no words in grammar" (54). "Grammar is a
conditional expanse" (55), which limits language by establishing rules
for the placement of words in the expanse of the sentence. The limitations imposed by grammar have to do with "continuity" (61), with
"origin" (95) and with "following after" (98), in other words with syn-
tagmatic relationships. Grammar makes language a temporal medium: "Grammar makes dates" (57), and "A sentence means that
there is a future" (71). Stein is inclined to think of language spatially.
For her the ideal sentence "makes not it told but it hold. A hold is
where they put things" (29). "A sentence has nothing to do about
words. . . . It has nothing to do with them" (142). Again, "every word
is at one time" (142). The ideal sentence is simply a "wedding," the
physical joining of words in space.

Everything Stein has to say about sentences in *How to Write* is
extended by analogy to paragraphs. A paragraph is composed of sentences, as a sentence is composed of words. Like a sentence, a paragraph should obey no rules. But what are the rules governing
paragraphs? They are certainly less rigid, less codified than the rules
of grammar. They are also therefore less abstract, less formal. A
paragraph expresses and develops an idea or an emotion, and its
form is determined only by the scope of the thought or feeling and
by the intentions of the writer. In the sense that they are emotive,

Stein calls paragraphs "emotional." But paragraphs not only "regis-
ter" emotions; they also "limit" them. Paragraphs set boundaries on
expression. The rules of paragraphing, although not as formalized as
those of grammar, dictate the length and the strategy of the paragraph—when to begin and when to end, and how to connect the sentences within it. Stein wants to do away with these rules. "A
paragraph is a liberty and a liberty is in between" (139). Not content
with saving the sentence, Stein wishes to liberate the paragraph. A
paragraph should be a "succession" or a "series of sentences" (136).
The "in between," the connection of the sentences in a paragraph,
and the rhetorical transitions which connect contiguous paragraphs,
should be eliminated. If a paragraph were merely a space in which to
arrange the "paraphanelia" of sentences (139), it would be neither a
limitation nor a development of those sentences. It would not sacrifice immediate expression to the demands of logical continuity, as
does the conventional paragraph. It would neither attenuate expression nor limit its unstructured flow. As the sentence should be a
"hold" for words, the paragraph should be a "hold" for sentences. In
fact, in *How to Write* there are no conventional paragraphs. The text
is divided into blocks of sentences, but as for units of expression,
Stein asserts "A sentence is our paragraph" (116).

According to Stein, sentences, unlike paragraphs, are not emotional. At the beginning of "Plays" Stein claims to have discovered in
How to Write this fundamental difference between paragraphs and
sentences:

In a book I wrote called How To Write I made a discovery which I considered fundamental, that sentences are not emotional and that paragraphs are.
I found out about language that paragraphs are emotional and sentences are
not and I found out something else about it. I found out that this difference
was not a contradiction but a combination and that this combination causes
one to think endlessly about sentences and paragraphs because the emotional
paragraphs are made up of unemotional sentences.[73]

It is in combination that unemotional sentences make emotional
paragraphs. The nature of individual units is altered when the units
combine to form larger units: "These are not sentences they are a
part of a paragraph" (167). Stein wished to preserve the identity of
the parts, to prevent the parts from merging, connecting, or combining. She did not wish to compromise the spatial integrity of each unit
by sacrificing it to the temporal flow of discourse. Her prescription
for "how to write" words and sentences so that they are "at one time"
is to avoid the natural tendency to make larger units accretions of
smaller units—sums of parts.

While she was working on *How to Write* and subsequently, Stein applied the instructions generated in *How to Write* to the writing of plays. In doing so, she had to come to terms with the difference between spoken and written language. As Roman Jakobson writes, "The former has a purely temporal character, whereas the latter connects time and space. While the sounds that we hear disappear, when we read we usually have immobile letters before us and the time of the written flow of words is reversible."[74] What Stein tries to do in her later lang-scape plays is to give the spoken language a spatial character. She had tried this once before in *A List* and its sister texts; in the lang-scape plays of the early thirties she proceeds along a different track toward the same goal. As she had opposed the momentum of performance in *Four Saints*, she now opposes the momentum of language to a degree that makes the text of *Four Saints* look like a model of coherence and continuity. Through extreme discontinuity and fragmentation on all levels of the text (side text, main text, and performance text), words and the moments of performance in which they are uttered do exist "one at a time." They are only here and now, connected to neither past nor future words and moments. The result of Stein's efforts is that many of these plays are difficult to comprehend and even more difficult to enact, even with "music to help them."[75]

"In order for the utterance to be understood," writes Jakobson, "attention to the flow of speech must be combined with moments of 'simultaneous synthesis.' . . . This is the process of unifying the elements that have already disappeared from immediate perception with those that already belong to memory. These elements are then combined into larger groupings: sounds into words, words into sentences, and sentences into utterances."[76] Naturally, plays that frustrate this process will not play well in the theater where they effectively turn away from the audience and its interpretive and affective response to the play. The least successful of these plays are those in which Stein simply follows the instructions of *How to Write*. The most successful are those in which she metadramatically considers the effect such a "program" for writing has on the performance event. In the final section of this chapter I discuss a number of these plays, some successful, some not, but all interesting for what they have to tell us about language in the theater.

VI

One of the first plays written "under the influence" of *How to Write* was *Paiseu. A Play. A Work of Pure Imagination in Which No Reminiscences Intrude.*[77] As its title suggests, it is about the *pays*: rural pursuits (sowing, reaping, winnowing); rural geography (clouds, trees, hill-sides, marshes, and gardens); and rural flora and fauna.[78] But it is about these subjects in the same way that *Four Saints* is about saints. In *Paiseu* Stein is far more preoccupied with names than she is with the bucolic setting and the homely activities she includes in her play. Names appear in almost every line of text. Here, as in *A Circular Play*, Stein does not give her "characters" any words to speak; this play too is composed entirely of authorial commentary. Yet the author is not alone; the country landscape is so filled with people it seems more a bustling city than the peaceful *pays*.

In her meditations on grammar in *How to Write*, Stein had not neglected names and their grammatical next of kin, nouns. She described a noun as "the name of anything" (130). But she objected to the reversal of the axiom: "A name and a noun is not the same that is a great discovery. A name is a place and a time a noun is once in a while" (207); "A name is not a noun because they will think that Ellen means something so it does for instance" (189). A name then has no "meaning" beyond the one instance of its application to a particular person or place. That makes a name an exciting and perfect word because it can never grow stale like the recurring noun. Because it comes "once in a while" a noun loses its correspondence to a particular place and time, loses its singularity and becomes a generalization, loses its concrete spatiality, as it were, and becomes an abstraction.

Previously, in *A List*, Stein had considered the relationship between a name in a play text and an object or person in performance. In that play Stein showed that the name is primordial, that the objects in the theater have no existence unless their names first exist in the text. In *Paiseu* she makes a similar claim for the primacy of names, but here she severs the connection between name and performance object. Here the names are objects themselves, and as such, they are not generalizable from one appearance to the next and thus cannot be represented continuously or recurrently during the performance.

As I noted earlier in my discussion of *A List*, a name in a play text corresponds to an imaginary being who exists only in the playwright's mind. The only way this imaginary being can become real, can exist in the performance, is through the text. He or she does this by speaking and by being spoken of. In *Paiseu* none of the names speak; so they cannot be known in that way. But they are spoken of. They are subjects in sentences where they are attached to predications about the person named. Thus, in *Paiseu* we hear of someone named Geronimo "in season," "invited," and "in rejoinder" (155–157). We learn, among other things, that "Geronimo makes a middle," that he "makes mended marshes," and that he "has all patience here" (158); we learn that he "is curiously careless"; that he "felt the need of our support" (159)—and much, much more. (Geronimo is the most fre-quently occurring name in the play.) However, Stein prevents us from generalizing from these particles of information about Geron-imo. Each predication is "at one time," without continuity, without eventual summation. Therefore, although it may perform the gram-matical function of a noun, the name retains its special status as a word without the accumulated, adherent meaning that normally comes from words in context.

Since the names in *Paiseu* correspond directly to the person named and have no generalized significance, they may be brought together spatially (in the "hold" of a sentence, for instance) without merging conceptually. Let us take the ubiquitous "Geronimo," for ex-ample. Geronimo is the given name of a "character" in *Paiseu*. Addi-tionally, the name Geronimo serves as a kind of surname for eighty other individuals in the play, as in Gerald Geronimo, Gabrielle Ge-ronimo, Joseph Geronimo, and Edgar Arthur Henry Edward Allen Russell Geronimo. The names Gerald, Joseph, Henry, Russell, and so on, represent separate "characters," referred to at least once by given name only.

A shared surname usually signifies a familial, ethnic, or categori-cal affinity among those who share it. Not so in *Paiseu*. The juxtapo-sition of names indicates nothing more than contiguity in a written text. The names Edgar Arthur Henry Edward Allen Russell Geron-imo take the singular verb "whistles" because they share the same space in the sentence; they are parts of a collective subject, the per-formers of a single activity—whistling. However, the proximity of the names does not blur the distinctions between them as singular ob-jects. If we imagine instead a sentence which reads, "Happy hand-some nervous blue-eyed pleasant Allen whistles," or "Son, brother, husband, expatriate, lawyer, neighbor Allen whistles," we can see the difference between names and other words. Each word in our two imaginary sentences contributes to a total concept that builds gradu-ally as the sentence proceeds; each word adds a new piece of infor-mation to the whole. This does not happen in the succession of names leading up to the verb "whistles." The names are together, but they do not merge. They do not "add up." For this reason, names are Stein's model words, exactly the kind of vocabulary she called for in *How to Write*.

As much as names in *Paiseu* frustrate synthesis and instrumen-tality, they are, nonetheless, parts of sentences and thus they do not escape from the inevitable linear movement that the sentence in-volves them in, especially when the sentences are spoken. In subse-quent plays Stein was to struggle not only against synthesis but also against linearity.

First she began to place periods after the subjects of her sentences, after the names. There is one such "sentence" in *Paiseu*: "Rudolph Geronimo. Is never mistaken" (158). This format was to become the mainstay of her plays of the early thirties. With a single mark of punctuation, the subject of the sentence becomes its speaker and the sentence is rendered incomplete. When an entire play is written in this way, the normal division of text into side text and main text forces an additional discontinuity—that between parts of a sentence. Each utterance in such a play is a fragment. The linear movement of the sentence is effectively disrupted by the conventional bifurcation of the play text.

As she uses the period to separate subject and predicate, speaker and utterance, Stein also uses it to fragment the spoken lines, as in the following from *They Must. Be Wedded. To Their Wife:*

Julia.	It is rightly. That is it. Or. That it is. Or that. Is it.
Josephine.	By which. They wish.
Julia.	And full of. Might they. Be. Without. A calling of. More than they. Further.
Josephine.	Should have thought likely.
Therese.	It is. A credit. And a pleasure.[79]

In this way Stein disrupts grammatical continuity and, if we imagine the appropriate breath stops at each period, slows the onrush of speech, allowing each word its full value as "vocabulary."

Stein often pursued such discontinuity to extreme lengths. For instance, again from *They Must. Be Wedded:*

Therese.	With their address.
Therese.	But which they will.
Therese.	But she. May be. Very well fitted.
Therese.	To be clothed. For the winter.
Therese.	To be. Admittedly. Not. In pretension.
Therese.	Nor as well. (237)

Since all six lines are spoken by Therese, the repetition of her name is an unnecessary and annoying intrusion for the reader. It is, however, extremely effective in disrupting the linear progress of language. Our pursuit of linear succession is thwarted by the repeated shifting of our eyes back to that superfluous but insistent name.

In writing, Stein could use punctuation and the physical placement of words on the page to interfere with spatial and grammatical linearity. The visual effect of Therese's name on the reader's rate and mode of comprehension can be matched in performance by the assignment of the various fragments of a sentence or a thought to several speakers, with a comparable effect on the listener. This promised to be far more reliable as a source of discontinuity in performance than the pause suggested by a period, and far more effective. In combination, as in the following from *They Must. Be Wedded*, the two devices successfully disrupt the natural continuity of utterance:

Therese.	She will.
Julia.	Adhere. To her family.
Therese.	She will.
Josephine.	Be even pleased.
Therese.	To have them come.
Josephine.	To have been. Left. To them.
Therese.	As they will manage.
Julia.	But which they.
Josephine.	Will suggest. (237)

Stein created entire plays out of this sort of "schizologue," where the human voice assists her in breaking up grammatical sentences into discontinuous segments.

Stein further thwarts the forward flow of natural utterance by making her performance text a patchwork of voices. In *They Must. Be Wedded* we find on a single page of text the following instructions for the combination, separation, and recombination of voices: Josephine and Therese speak at once, then Josephine and Julia, followed by Julia and Therese, Therese again with Josephine, and then again with Julia. Julia and Ernest then join voices and are eventually joined by Therese (213–214). The fragmentation of the written text has in this way a corresponding vocal fragmentation. The names are not only seen, as words on a page, but are heard as voices speaking in constantly shifting configurations. (This idea may have been suggested to Stein in part by Virgil Thomson's scoring of her texts for various voices and by his insistence in *Four Saints* on the necessity of parceling out speeches, breaking them up for greater musical interest.)

Not only does Stein specify shifts in the combination of voices, she also indicates that there will be shifts in the speaker-listener relationship. So, for example, we have the following sequence: Josephine speaks, then Therese; Josephine then speaks to Therese; Therese and Francis speak simultaneously, then Therese alone addresses Josephine; Josephine in turn addresses Ernest and then John (214). To be noticeable, this designation of speaker and listener must be indicated in performance by some sort of physical shift of attention. Therese must turn away from Ernest to John, or perform some equivalent action, in order to inform the audience that she means to address her remarks to one and not to the other. In both the shifting of vocal combinations and the shifting of attention, the written "poetry" of character names translates into a poetry of performance. The actors in these plays serve to convey Steinian grammar and poetry and to create a performance as discontinuous as the written text from which it is extracted.

Stein also uses setting to the same effect. In a play ironically called *An Historic Drama in Memory of Winnie Elliot* Stein uses incessant scene changes to intensify the fragmentation caused by the rapid alternation of voices. This play is one of a trilogy with *Second Historic Drama. In the Country* and *Third Historic Drama.* Stein will have her fun with us, calling dramas in which temporal continuity is thwarted "historic," invoking memory and sequence in the titles of three plays where nothing continues from one to the other except character names. A brief glance at Act 1 of the first play of the trilogy and a catalogue of the changes in scene which take place within forty-four lines of text are a sufficient demonstration of Stein's method. Scene changes occur with the following frequency: the act opens "Inside of a room" (three lines of speech follow), then "Leaving together" (two lines of speech), "Out of the house" (eight lines of speech), "In the house" (seven lines of speech), "A street where they are building" (four lines of speech), "A building which is not finished" (seven lines of speech), "After they left" (four lines of speech), "Partly at the door" (four lines of speech), "At the door" (five lines of speech).[80] This pace continues unabated through all three plays of the trilogy.

Like the periods she uses so liberally throughout her texts, setting and character are no more than arbitrary textual divisions. Should we fail to notice that Stein has reduced characters to mere textual divisions, she gives us several plays in which character names are moved to center page, so that the text looks like this:

George L.

I know I sit and will
They know their care
For me.
She thinks it is
And better than they can
With wives be theirs.
Have had a ground.

George M.

Out likely in a minute
Leave it clear.[81]

This placement of the character names reminds us of Stein's method
of indicating act/scene divisions, as in:

Scene II

Therese. May talk. Of it.

In fact, in *They Weighed Weighed-Layed*, Stein makes the connection
between character and act or scene divisions even more obvious by
giving us characters named Maurice I, Maurice II, Maurice III, Maurice IV. Voices combine, separate and recombine, but the names are,
with one exception, followed by roman numerals and always placed
center page above the text to be spoken.[82]

In all the plays I have been discussing, and in many others of the
same period, Stein tried, as she did in *Four Saints*, to make time stand
still in the theater. She treats the performance text like a written text,
striving not for natural utterance or for word music but for a condition approaching the potential immobility of a written text where
each word can exist "at one time." The play is a frame for language
(a lang-scape); the performance exhibits the language to the audience, one bit at a time. No synthesis is possible. Most of these plays
would try the patience of an audience because they fight the very
nature of utterance and performance and therefore frustrate the
expectations and normal activities of the spectator. If these plays tell
us anything about theater, it is that in the theater more than in any
other medium, time cannot be vanquished.

Stein's names will be attached to actors, and they will speak and
act as is their wont. As she writes in *A Manoir*, "All the characters
come in and are eventful."[83] They "come and go," "commence to
mingle and gather," do "a great deal of work," and all of this activity
"introduces conversation" (278–279). Like the play which is a static
object (a text), "A manoir may be built of stones and covered with
mortar," may simply be an edifice (285). But a play is also a home for
actors, as a manoir is "a house for a gentleman" (281), "a temporary
home" (279). Once Stein's play is inhabited (performed), it is ani-
mated. Because of the actors, performance is eventful; it involves the
immobile text in history, which Stein reminds herself in *A Manoir*,
"takes time" and "makes memory" (279). Language in performance,
even Gertrude Stein's language, is "historic" after all.

Chapter 3

On Plays and Playing: 1934 to 1937

In the summer of 1934 Gertrude Stein wrote six lectures for her up-coming lecture tour of the United States. The preparation of these lectures and the tour itself led her to begin a self-examination that would last until the end of her life. In the public lectures (which, in addition to *Lectures in America*, included *Composition as Explanation* and *Narration*), Stein looked back at work already written, reflected on genres in which she had worked, and discussed media with which she was familiar. These public lectures convey Stein's belief that what she had aimed for she had accomplished, that what she had accomplished had enduring significance. She was certain that what she knew about literature and art were the "truths" of those media and that, if we would but understand what she was telling us, we too would know the truth. Her lectures, her public accounts, are like stories of "what happened" in her own aesthetic development and in the develop-ment of whatever subject she was discussing—fiction, poetry, paint-ing. As stories they have a relatively tidy progression toward the happy ending of discovery and aesthetic advancement. They are like a general's stories of successful battles waged and won, stories that leave out any account of the bloody casualties. In Stein's private writ-ing of the same period, which is equally self-reflexive and self-evaluative, the bodies are everywhere and the war is not yet won.

In this chapter, I will be discussing "Plays," one of the public vic-tory commemorations included in *Lectures in America* and presented at various stops on the 1934–1935 tour, and *The Geographical History of America*, a private meditation written in 1935, after the tour, after the last hurrah, a look behind the scenes at a war still in progress. Both texts deal with playwriting, though each gives a different ac-count.

I

In "Plays" the story follows the pattern of problem/resolution. Gertrude Stein realized that there were problems with the way language was used in the theater; Gertrude Stein wrote plays that resolved those problems. She tells her story primarily from the point of view of a theatergoer. Almost everything she knows about theater she learned as a member of the audience. She writes her story of a spectator's life in the theater so that it recapitulates the history of the theater as a medium, thereby universalizing her perceptions. If we, her own audience, pay attention to what the history of theater teaches us, we will arrive at the same conclusions that Gertrude Stein arrived at in the course of her own history in the theater. Anybody's autobiography is, by extension, everybody's autobiography: before she begins her story, she tells us, "All this is very important, and important for me and important, just important. It has of course a great deal to do with the theatre a great great deal,"[1] and later, she says,"I think this is fairly everybody's experience and it was completely mine" (112).

Her experience began when, as a small child, she attended plays and operas in San Francisco. In her story, she transforms plays into spectacles and theaters into arenas:

Generally speaking all the early recollections all a child's feeling of the theatre is two things. One which is in a way like a circus that is the general movement and light and air which any theatre has, and a great deal of glitter in the light and a great deal of height in the air, and then there are moments, a very very few moments but still moments. (112)

From this primitive conception of the theater as a locus of excitement, Stein matured to a consciousness of the stage as a visual focus distinct from the place which encloses it, and of the maneuvers on that stage as a performance separate from the activities of the audience. (She noticed first the movement of an inanimate prop, the block of ice in *Uncle Tom's Cabin*, and then the movement of people in the duel in *Faust* and in the battle in the Buffalo Bill Indian show.) The similarity of her account to anthropological conjectures of the origins of drama is striking. From a spontaneous gathering of people, all moving in celebration, to the demarcation of an area in which to celebrate, to the designation of certain members of the community as performers, to the use of masks, props, and ritualized movement to re-create an episode in the life of the tribe (likely to be a hunt or a fight)—the pattern of the theater's origins and growth is embodied in Gertrude Stein's experience.

In none of Stein's theater memories to this point does language intrude. Just as theater itself is rooted in dance and nonverbal ritual, so Stein's re-creation of her own theater roots begins with physical, not linguistic, experiences. Dramatic "poetry" probably made its first appearance as a rhythmic accompaniment to dance, an emotive gesture. In Stein's narrative, too, language first surfaces as a cry:

In spite of my having seen operas quite often the first thing that I remember as sound on the stage was the playing by some English actor of Richelieu at the Oakland theatre and his repeated calling out, Nemours Nemours. That is the first thing that I remember hearing with my ears at the theatre. (113)

Concurrent with her awareness of language was Stein's realization that play and performance are forms of art, not manifestations of real life. The cry "Nemours" came from an English actor playing Richelieu. The play Stein remembers most vividly from this period is *Hamlet*, and the focus of her memory is on the device of the play within the play and on Hamlet as spectator.

Stein next introduces the reading of plays into her history. As she began reading plays, she understood that the action on the stage was not improvised and unpredictable, but that it was dictated by the poetry written prior to the performance. She understood, that is, that the language of a preexisting text had created the story and the characters which were presented in the theater.

At this point in her lecture, Stein has set the scene, so to speak, with all the elements of theater, introduced in the order of their historical appearance. These elements (community and spectatorship, theater as enclosure, stage as focal point, spectacle, action, actors, language, art, and the poetry, plot, and character created by the written text) did not coalesce for Stein until adolescence, "when one does really live in a whole play"(112). The glue which fused the parts was her acceptance of the dramatic illusion, her acquiescence to the convention that drama is an imitation of life. Her enjoyment of the performance required her to forget the artfulness of the drama and to believe that the play was real, or at least, realistic, and that what was represented in the play corresponded to some reality in the spectator's life.

Then the next thing I knew was adolescence and going to the theatre all the time, a great deal alone, and all of it making an outside inside existence for me . . . so real that it the theatre made me real outside of me which up to that time I never had been in my emotion. (114)

Stein's adolescent belief in the reality of the theater event is analogous to the naïve (adolescent, if you will) obsession with illusionism in the theater.[2]

Though, as an adolescent, Stein was caught up in the realism of the theater event, she eventually rejected the mimetic premise behind illusionism, that drama imitates life and that, therefore, the stage should re-create the external forms of the real world as faithfully as possible. The curtain itself tells us that life and the theater are separate:

In the first place at the theatre there is the curtain and the curtain already makes one feel that one is not going to have the same tempo as the thing that is there behind the curtain. The emotion of you on one side of the curtain and what is on the other side of the curtain are not going to be going on together. (95)

The spectator belongs to a different time zone than do the actors on the stage. He moves at a different tempo, though a naïve spectator might forget this difference as Stein and her brother did at a performance of *Lohengrin*:

And then there was Lohengrin, and there all that I saw was the swan being changed into a boy, our insisting on seeing that made my father with us lose the last boat home to Oakland, but my brother and I did not mind, naturally not as it was the moment. (113)

According to Stein, the main difference between our experience of the theater and our experience of real life is that the theater, no matter how it moves and excites us in "the moment," usually denies us the fundamental prerogative of life—participation. In the theater we are spectators, not actors. The theater is that "at which one looks on"; life is "a scene in which one takes part or an action in which one takes part" (99). Even if we are only witnesses to real events, our involvement in them will be more complete than it is in theatrical events because we bring to real actions a familiarity with preceding actions and with the actors, which, says Stein, can never be attained in an evening of theater:

In ordinary life one has known pretty well the people with whom one is having the exciting scene before the exciting scene takes place and one of the most exciting elements in the excitement be it love or a quarrel or a struggle is that, that having been well known that is familiarly known, they all act in acting violently act in the same way as they always did. . . .
It is not possible in the theatre to produce familiarity which is of the essence of acquaintance because, in the first place when the actors are there they are there and they are there right away. (108–109)

A written narrative of an action, on the other hand, provides the progressive familiarity which Stein found wanting in the theater. In that respect fiction more closely approximates life than does dramatic action. However, fiction also provides a kind of control over the temporal unfolding of events which dramatic action and life do not, except in retrospect.

In the exciting story, you so to speak have control of it as you have in your memory of a really exciting scene, it is not as it is on the stage a thing over which you have no real control. You can with an exciting story find out the end and so begin over again . . . but the stage is different. . . . No matter how well you know the end of the stage story it is nevertheless not within your control. (98)

One can adjust the tempo of a written narrative, and one can repeat bits of it at will. One can stop it in order to puzzle over it; one can avoid it indefinitely; one can experience it in any order one chooses. But theater, like life, compels us, even against our will; and thus, as Stein acknowledges, theater offers us lifelike excitement.

A written narrative also differs from a dramatic action in one other respect: in performance the language of the dramatic text is not seen, but heard. For Stein, in attendance at conventional dramatic performances, the visual elements (the action and scenic design) and the spoken language seemed incompatible. One set of stimuli interfered with the other:

I became fairly consciously troubled by the things over which one stumbles over which one stumbled to such an extent that the time of one's emotion in relation to the scene was always interrupted. The things over which one stumbled and there it was a matter both of seeing and of hearing were clothes, voices, what they the actors said, how they were dressed and how that related itself to their moving around. . . . Then I began to vaguely wonder whether I could see and hear at the same time and which helped or interfered with the other. (114–115)

Visual perception in the theater moves linearly through the time of the performance, but the line is a broken one, a series of segments, a succession of present moments where what we see at the moment is independent of what we have just seen or will be seeing in the next moment. The moments are contiguous but not necessarily connected. Aural perception can also be a linear succession of present moments, but that is not how language works in conventional drama. The movement of language in the conventional Western play can best be represented by an unbroken, unidirectional arc. According to Stein, if the spectator tries to follow the arc, he will be distracted by the broken line of visual perception. But if he or she succumbs to the attraction of visual stimuli, he or she will fail to follow and understand the arc. In other words, to make sense is to dilute the effect of sensation, but to enjoy sensation is to become confused about meaning.

To further complicate matters, the mind (consciousness, in this case, not intellect) does not move linearly, but tangentially. Thus, any segment of the broken line or the arc could send the mind on a tangent. The components of the theatrical experience as Stein imagined it can be represented graphically:

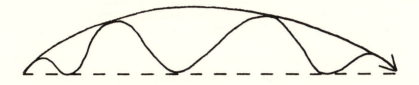

The spectator's meandering attention intermittently intersects both the text and the spectacle. When consciousness intersects the dramatic arc of the text, however, it may be difficult for the spectator to understand the plot, or the identity and motivation of characters, since each moment on the arc depends for meaning on its connection to preceding and subsequent moments. As Stein understands it, the play, a linguistic construct, never proceeds at the same tempo as the spectator's emotional and sensational experience of its enactment in the theater:

Your sensation as one in the audience in relation to the play played before you your sensation I say your emotion concerning that play is always either behind or ahead of the play at which you are looking and to which you are listening. So your emotion as a member of the audience is never going on at the same time as the action of the play. (93)

Most spectators are accustomed to the simultaneity of visual and aural stimuli in the theater, to the sensation of each moment fully occupied at the same time that it moves forward to the next moment. Nevertheless, there are times, as Jindřich Honzl notes, when one or more of the components of theater art "submerges below the surface of the spectator's conscious attention."[3] As Stein understood, the theater encompasses competing modes of perception, competing fields of attention, and competing rhythms of movement through time.

According to Stein, the conflict between the rhythms of consciousness, which dictate audience response, the succession of physical stimuli, and the progression of language in the service of plot and characterization produces a "nervousness" in the spectator. From her point of view, the end of a play is a relief, the removal of a burden, the cessation of an irritation. In comparison, at the end of a real event, we have feelings of completion and perfection:

If you are taking part in an actual violent scene, and you talk and they or he or she talk and it goes on and it gets more exciting and finally then it happens, whatever it is that does happen then when it happens then at the moment of happening is it a relief from the excitement or is it a completion of the excitement. In the real thing it is a completion of the excitement, in the theatre it is a relief from the excitement, and in that difference the difference between completion and relief is the difference between emotion concerning a thing seen on the stage and the emotion concerning a real presentation that is really something happening. (96–97)

To illustrate this point, Stein quotes from her novel *The Making of Americans*. The excerpt she uses contains an important clue to the motivation behind, and the paradox inherent in, Stein's plays:

This one, and the one I am now beginning describing is Martha Hersland and this is a little story of the acting in her of her being in her very young living, this one was a very little one then and she was running and she was in the street and it was a muddy one and she had an umbrella that she was dragging and she was crying. I will throw the umbrella in the mud, she was saying, she was very little then, she was just beginning her schooling, I will throw the umbrella in the mud, she said and no one was near her and she was dragging the umbrella and bitterness possessed her, I will throw the umbrella in the mud, she was saying and nobody heard her, the others had run ahead to get home and they had left her, I will throw the umbrella in the mud, and there was desperate anger in her, I have throwed the umbrella in the mud, burst from her, she had thrown the umbrella in the mud and that was the end of it all in her. She had thrown the umbrella in the mud and no one heard her as it burst from her, I have throwed the umbrella in the mud, it was the end of all that to her. (97)

The central action of this paragraph, throwing the umbrella in the mud, is not described in the moment of its happening. "I will throw the umbrella in the mud," Martha says four times; then "I have throwed the umbrella in the mud," and so on. The action is predicted and recounted, but as it is done, it is unarticulated action, action without words: "No one heard it as it burst from her." This is action in life: words can describe its intention; words can describe its completion; but description will only suffice before or after, not during the event. The present moment is sensation and action, not verbalization. And Stein cautions us, "The business of Art . . . is to live in the actual present, that is the complete actual present, and to completely express that complete actual present" (104–105).

Can there be a kind of language in the theater which would not interfere with the "perfection" of action, or must language always create an "irritation," a "burden," and be a less immediate component of the theater experience than gesture? This is the question that bothered Stein when she attended plays, and that later concerned her in writing plays. At sixteen, Stein had a theater experience which suggested a possible answer to the question. She saw Sarah Bernhardt perform in San Francisco:

I must have been about sixteen years old and Bernhardt came to San Francisco and stayed two months. I knew a little french of course but really it did not matter, it was all so foreign and her voice being so varied and it all being so french I could rest in it untroubled. And I did. (115)

Since the play was in a foreign language which Stein did not fully understand, the words could not be a source of information about the characters or the plot. The sensuality of the language replaced its sense, and thus, language became just another of the physical stimuli of performance. In this way the problems created by the conflict between the rhythm of the spectator's consciousness and her enjoyment of the play's language could be eliminated. Normally, we listen to the language of a play in order to understand how the immediate utterance is connected to preceding and subsequent events and utterances on the dramatic arc. In that case, seeing, hearing, and response cannot coincide because hearing becomes a function of the intellect, busy with the acquisition of information through the vehicle of language for the purpose of comprehending the whole of the play. But when one doesn't understand the language to begin with, there is no "competition" between text and performance. As Stein described the experience:

It was better than the opera because it went on. It was better than the theatre because you did not have to get acquainted. The manners and customs of the french theatre created a thing in itself and it existed in and for itself as the poetical plays had that I used so much to read, there were so many characters just as there were in those plays and you did not have to know them they were so foreign, and the foreign scenery and actuality replaced the poetry and the voices replaced the portraits. It was for me a very simple direct and moving pleasure. (115–116)

Stein discovered that the most satisfactory theater experience for her was one in which language was no more nor less expressive than gesture, where the voices of characters replaced the portraits of them which their words normally convey, and where an experience of the playing replaced an understanding of the play.

Having made this discovery, Stein claimed to have discontinued attendance at plays in favor of opera and melodrama, the only kinds of theater she was able to enjoy at that point. The charm of opera for Stein, the playgoer, was its use of language for expression and melodic beauty more than for information. (One may suppose, though Stein does not say so, that opera's charm was only further enhanced by its customary presentation in a foreign language.) The attraction of melodrama derived from a similar use of language coming in part from the form's musical roots, and in part from its predictable format which alleviated Stein's need to garner information from the dialogue. In other words, both forms created the kind of situation created by the Bernhardt play.

After exhausting her pleasure in opera and melodrama, Stein abandoned the theater entirely, a move that coincided with a more drastic move, Stein's permanent expatriation to Paris in 1903. "Then I came to Paris to live and there for a long time I did not go to the theatre at all. I forgot the theatre, I never thought about the theatre" (117). Since Stein's history in the theater is analogous to the history of the theater as a medium, her sudden obliviousness to it is comparable to its disappearance as an evolving art form. By orchestrating the events of her narrative so that the theater stopped evolving during the years in which she assisted at the birth of modernism, revolutionizing narrative with *Melanctha* and poetry with *Tender Buttons*, she can emerge as the heroine of the story she tells in "Plays," the playwright who writes plays that are not stories ("anything that was not a story could be a play") and resolves forever the problem that arises when language is used as an instrument rather than an object.

In her first plays (the conversation plays, discussed in chapter 1), Stein had eliminated stories but had still tried to represent, through speech, "the essence of what happened" as well as the relations among individual speakers. However, in writing conversation plays, she reached a kind of dead end. "And then I had for the moment gone as far as I could then go in plays and I went back to poetry and portraits and description" (122). According to Stein, her breakthrough in the writing of plays came when she began to write "landscapes" and to think of a play as a "landscape":

I felt that if a play was exactly like a landscape then there would be no difficulty about the emotion of the person looking on at the play being behind or ahead of the play because the landscape does not have to make acquaintance.
    . . . The landscape has its formation and as after all a play has to have formation and be in relation one thing to the other thing and as the story is not the thing as any one is always telling something then the landscape not moving but being always in relation, . . . of that relation I wanted to make a play and I did, a great number of plays. (122–125)

Stein writes that *Four Saints* is the quintessential landscape play and is proof of her success at writing the kind of play that seemed called for by her previous dissatisfaction with the theater:

> Anyway I did write Four Saints an Opera to be Sung and I think it did almost what I wanted, it made a landscape and the movement in it was like a movement in and out with which anybody looking on can keep in time. . . .
>
> Anyway the play as I see it is exciting and it moves but it also stays and that is as I said in the beginning might be what a play should do.
>
> Anyway I am pleased. People write me that they are having a good time while the opera is going on a thing which they say does not very often happen to them at the theatre. (131)

With this verbal pat on the back Stein ends her lecture.

II

Between the writing of "Plays," a lecture for public consumption, and the writing of *The Geographical History of America*, a meditation for private enlightenment (though it was eventually published), Stein toured the United States, became a nationally recognized celebrity, and attended her first and only performance of *Four Saints*. (She had previously heard parts of it sung by Thomson accompanying himself on the piano.) Of this performance of her landscape play in which things were supposed to move but also to stay still, Stein wrote, "The movement was everything."[4] This was bound to have been an unsettling realization for her, but not nearly as unsettling as the fact that she was being valued and celebrated in her homeland as the writer of remarks (*The Autobiography of Alice B. Toklas* and her lectures) not literature. Her serious writing, her literature, was still not read, appreciated, or understood, while work she did not value, work written to earn money, was immensely popular and had made her too, at long last, immensely popular. The connection between writing as a private act and writing as a public product is the primary subject of *The Geographical History of America*. In this book she also ponders what she was trying to do in writing plays and how well she was able to do it.

The subtitle of *The Geographical History* is *The Relation of Human Nature to the Human Mind*. In Stein's system, human nature (which she also calls identity) is that part of us which is easily recognized and known, our surface selves, including our names and physical characteristics, the appurtenances, qualities, and actions by which we can be identified as social beings, and which change with time and pass out

of existence with our deaths. The human mind (entity) is more difficult for Stein to define. She declares that it is unchanging and timeless. It is what we really are and what we will always be. But what is
it? The question is not easily answered because the human mind is
seldom articulated. It may in fact be a pre-verbal phenomenon, but
we will never know if this is so because we only "know" through language. "Whether or whether not the human mind could exist if there
had been no human speech this I do not know." As we know it then,
the human mind is bound to be expressed verbally. Stein came to feel
that the mind is better represented by writing than by speech. She
writes:

But this I do know that the human mind is not the same thing as human
speech . . . writing has nothing to do with human speech with human nature
and therefore and therefore it has something to do with the human mind.[5]

While writing can "have something to do with" the human mind, not
all writing does. According to Stein, writing that is concerned with
the social activities of human beings does not reflect the mind; neither does writing that imitates the expressive vehicle of human nature, human speech. "Think anything you say has to do with human
nature and if you write what you say if you write what you do what is
done then it has to do with human nature and human nature is occupying but it is not interesting" (149–150). Stein laments, "I wish I
could say that talking had to do with the human mind I wish I could
say so" (66). But she cannot and she does not.

Stein notes repeatedly that "the human mind does play" (99)
and, conversely, that "human nature does not play" (100). In his
book, *Homo Ludens*, J. Huizinga reminds us that language-making is
an activity "permeated with play":

In the making of speech and language the spirit is continually "sparking"
between matter and mind, as it were, playing with this wondrous nominative
faculty. Behind every abstract expression there lie the boldest of metaphors,
and every metaphor is a play upon words. Thus in giving expression to life
man creates a second, poetic world alongside the world of nature.[6]

As a "grammarian" Stein had attempted to restore the original relationship between matter and mind, the original nominative and expressive function of language, so that it could again be poetic. The
steps Stein took in *How to Write* to save the sentence and liberate the
paragraph indicate that she hoped to create literature from the play
of her mind. The incorporation of mistakes, the freedom from the

logic of syntax, the digressive, tangential and often purposeless quality of her writing—these were all calculated to allow the mind to express freely its reaction to the world. The resulting poetry is often playful: full of riddles, songs, rhymes, puns, homophonic wordplay, secret codes, linguistic jokes, nonsensical but joyful word capers, and literary clues which tease us into false interpretive starts.

Huizinga describes the relationship between play and poetry as follows:

Poiesis . . . is a play-function. It proceeds within the play-ground of the mind, in a world of its own which the mind creates for it. There things have a very different physiognomy from the one they wear in "ordinary life," and are bound by ties other than those of logic and causality.[7]

Stein herself recognized and valued the connection between play and poetry, and their mutual freedom from the laws of logic and causality. She believed that her mind (because she was a poet) was a bridge between reality and language, not that she should use language to describe a reality perceived, but that she should incarnate reality by expressing with language the recreation of her mind as it absorbed and reflected on the outside world. In reading Gertrude Stein as she hoped she would be read, we are supposed to see her at play and to have contact with the world she perceives by having contact with her playful language, to participate in the original experience of naming, of applying words to experience so that words and what they represent inhabit the same moment in time.

In writing plays, Stein was trying to establish a similar connection between the play as a text and the original moment of play in which the text was created, to make the player and her play present in the play. In *Byron*, a play she wrote just before embarking on her lecture tour, she writes: "They watch me as they watch this. There we are as they watch this."[8] As the play is performed the original player will be present—so Stein believed as she wrote *Byron*. But after "watching" a performance in which "the movement was everything," she no longer seemed certain that her mind and its playful expression through language were there in the play that she watched. When she was writing it, the text had been Stein's play, the recreation and re-creation of her mind. What became of that play in the theater event of which it was only a part? Once it was used as a source for the performance, the play was no longer the exclusive expression or property of Gertrude Stein. At the time of performance, Stein was no longer playing. Furthermore, the written text, which for Stein had been the articulation of a spontaneous linguistic playfulness in the presence of the

phenomenal world, was no longer spontaneous and no longer syn-
chronous with the writer's playful moment. Performance is a rehearsed and repeated enactment. Ritualized and, in a sense, fossilized
through repetition (memorized, remembered), the text was no longer
immediate. It was no longer the game itself, but rather the book of
rules.

Stein was confronting an antithesis inherent in the theater: the
conflict between the playwright's freedom to play and her obligation
to modify that play according to the norms and the requirements of
theatrical realization. As Donald Baker explains:

On the one hand, then, play as exploration is essentially self-expressive and
improvisational, and, on the other, with the repetition and rehearsal of improvisations that are satisfying to the individual and receive the approval of
the individual's community, it appears as ritualization of experience in the
act of consolidating personal behavior patterns and social norms.[9]

Stein balked at the necessity of ritualizing her own playful and personal verbal explorations, balked at the transformation of play into
ritual. Her doubts about the possibility of transferring the play of the
mind, through the words of a play, into the theater are expressed
again and again in *The Geographical History*.

Several of Stein's stipulations regarding the human mind at play
are incompatible with writing for the theater. In the first place, Stein
declares that the "human mind lives alone" (196). "There is no chorus in the human mind" (109). The human mind has only one voice,
its own, and that voice is not projected to an audience. Play is not
audience-directed, although it may have an audience. Whereas human nature "announces itself," "the writing that is the human mind
does not consist in messages" (116). "Nobody sees the human mind
while it is being existing" (182). Regarding the privacy of the human
mind, Stein writes, "The human mind cannot find out but it is in it is
not out. If the human mind is in then it is not out" (121); and "there
are no witnesses to the autobiography of any one that has a human
mind" (90). By turning play into "a play," Stein was publicizing what
was supposed to be a very private act.

Furthermore, by turning play into "a play," Stein was dragging
the mind into time, despite her contention that the mind and its play
are timeless:

I then no longer [after writing *The Making of Americans*] was worrying about
time but I just stopped going on. That is what time is. There is always enough
and so there is no going on no not in the human mind there is just staying
within. . . . The human mind had nothing to do with time. (192–193)

If the human mind has nothing to do with time, neither does it have to do with history and remembering. Time was Stein's long-standing enemy, and in her public lecture on plays she claimed that in writing landscape plays she had successfully stopped time. But the play, once written, is historical, and it must be remembered in order to be repeated in performance.

How can the conflict between playing and the play be resolved? On page 100 of *The Geographical History*, Stein proposes to "make a play with just the human mind." "Let us try," she invites us. The play of the human mind is this:

A Play.
Make. There is no place to wait.
Wilder. Made is not past make.
Call it all to order because perhaps here there has not been it all kept entirely in the human mind.
And so to begin again.
Make. No instance of make.
Wilder. Do not change wild to wilder.

This snippet of writing concentrates on its own composition; it is a dialogue, as it were, between creator and creation. If the play is not kept entirely in the human mind, it must begin again. In the play of the mind, there is no waiting, no past tense, no instance, no change, no comparative adjective; in other words, there are no temporal functions.[10]

Next Stein offers a play of human nature:

Now make a play with human nature and not anything of the human mind.
Pivoines smell like magnolias.
Dogs smell like dogs.
Men smell like men.
And gardens smell differently at different seasons of the year.
This is a mistake this is not human nature it comes more nearly having to do with the human mind.
Try a play again. (100–101)

The play of human nature has to do with comparisons and resemblances, with making connections between one thing and another. Stein's similes are predictably circular, but the fact remains that human nature seeks resemblances, even if it fails to find them, while the human mind revels in difference. To find similarity is to cross the boundaries of time and space which separate objects:

In the human mind there is no identity and place and time but in money and romanticism and question and answer a little something yes that is not human nature but has something that is space and time and identity. (237)

Singularity—entity—is not a function of time. At each instant, the human mind is what it is. It is not generalizable. Thus, Stein's comment about gardens, that they "smell differently at different seasons of the year," nearly turns the play of human nature, a play about resemblances, into a play of the human mind, a play about difference.

The ideal play, in Stein's system, should focus on the mind of its creator and the process of its own creation. It should be singular, something outside time, unrepeatable. In this way it will be a true product of the mind, a true masterpiece. But as Stein notes in *The Geographical History*, this ideal is difficult to realize. Once writing is written it is no longer private and timeless:

I wish writing would not sound like writing and yet what else can any writing sound like.

Well yes it can it cannot sound like writing because if it sounds like writing then anybody can see it being written, and the human mind nobody sees the human mind while it is being existing, and master-pieces well master-pieces may not be other than that that they do not exist as anybody seeing them and yet there they are. (182)

If the human mind and masterpieces should not be seen, then the publication and the performance of writing separate it even further from the mind. "As long as nothing or very little that you write is published it is all sacred but after a great deal of it is published is it everything that you write is it as sacred" (61).

The secularization of writing can occur even when the writer does not intend it, and even when the writing was sacred prior to publication. In most of her work Stein could make a comforting distinction between that which was intended for publication, like *The Autobiography of Alice B. Toklas*, that which was originally sacred but then published, and that which was never seen, so always sacred. The writing of plays, however, does not allow such fine distinctions. Whatever the philosophy of pure mental play behind its composition, a play is anything but a private matter. Eventual performance, with its attendant publicity, is the ultimate fate of the play. Although Stein had written many plays in which she explored and resolved the tension between the static text and the dynamic performance, and the conflict between poiesis and playwriting, *The Geographical History* suggests that she was no longer convinced of the possibility of reconciling her own poetic process and product with playwriting and with the performance of her play.

III

In the year following the completion of *The Geographical History*, Stein wrote only two plays, *Listen to Me* and *A Play Called Not and Now*. On the surface the two texts could not be more dissimilar. *Listen to Me* is in the style of *Four Saints*. *Not and Now* is more like a narrative than a play—narrative voice, past tense, indirect discourse. Yet both plays manifest the misgivings about playwriting that Stein had articulated in her discussion of play in *The Geographical History*.

Not and Now was inspired by a cocktail party given in Stein's honor two years earlier in Hollywood. Attended by movie stars and other luminaries, the party had crystallized Stein's worries about the transformation she was undergoing from a private to a public self. From observing other celebrities she had determined that there was an enormous gap between the projected self (who is almost a character) and the self hidden from view. Though the public self bears the same name and physical characteristics, she is not the private self, only a reasonable facsimile. So too the characters in a play may resemble or represent real people, but they are not before us as real people. Stein makes her point immediately in her character list, which reads:

Characters
A man who looks like Dashiell Hammett
A man who looks like Picasso
A man who looks like Charlie Chaplin
A man who looks like Lord Berners
and a man who looks like David Green.
Women
A woman who looks like Anita Loos
A woman who looks like Gertrude Atherton
A woman who looks like Lady Diana Grey
A woman who looks like Katharine Cornell
A woman who looks like Daisy Fellowes
A woman who looks like Mrs. Andrew Greene[11]

This formula, "the man" or "the one" or "the woman" who looks like so-and-so, is used without exception throughout the play every time a character is mentioned. The public self (character) we see might confuse us by its resemblance to the private self (real person), but Stein's language never allows us to forget that a character is not a real person, that a public self is not a real self.

In Scene 3, however, Stein refers to a "mysterious assemblage of women." These women, she tells us, do not look like anyone:

> The mysterious assemblage of women did not look like Gertrude Atherton and Anita Loos Lady Diana Grey Katharine Cornell and Daisy Fellowes, they did not look at all like them not at all, *they did not look like a mysterious assemblage of women, they were a mysterious assemblage of women* and they all were in their ordinary clothes and sitting down in chairs under a shelter in the Luxembourg Gardens, there were no men or children with them. (430) (emphasis added)

There are many reasons for making an exception of these women from the "looks like" formula. They are not celebrities (they have no names and no public identity); we know very little about them (they are "mysterious," coming as they do without biographies); they are not individuated ("an assemblage"); and they play no social role (having no children or men around them, they cannot be classified as mothers or wives). However, they do appear in Stein's play. Are they not, then, automatically "like" a mysterious assemblage of women by Stein's own standards? The fact is that Stein excludes them from the performance of her play. They are simply a group that is told about in the play. They were sitting in the Luxembourg Gardens when Stein wrote this account of them; they are, for all we know, still sitting there. Since the real women are not actively incorporated into the imagined world of the play as characters, they are still real. Once an object, event, or person is reproduced in a play (not just told about but actually presented), it is no longer real but only resembles reality.

The play that settles for resemblance and represents a social reality in an imagined world was to Stein's way of thinking a play of, by, and for human nature. It would therefore be time-bound rather than timeless. It would not be able to occupy the immediate present of performance time because it would be connected to a sphere of life which is automatically dated. *Not and Now* is such a play, and though it begins in the present tense—"These are the characters and this is what they do. . . . They move and speak,"—it quickly changes to past tense. On the second page of text Stein writes, "The one that looked like Dashiell Hammett said he was saying yes." This line initiates a paragraph set entirely in the past tense. Stein approves of the new mode. "That is it," she announces. "And so they all began again to look like another one." Thereafter, Stein uses the past tense almost exclusively. Her insistence on the narrative "pastness" of her play points to the discrepancy between the immediacy of performance and the "deadness" of a play text which draws on a world outside the work of art. But *Not and Now* also demonstrates that even when a play text is simply the record of the dramatist's imaginative playing with language, it cannot compete with those objects and acts and people that "play" during performance. Writing makes language a product, removes it from the process of its own creation. As she writes in *Composition as Explanation*, "The quality in the creation of expression the quality in a composition that makes it go dead just after it has been made is very troublesome."[12] Nowhere is this "deadness" of written compositions more obvious than in the theater because performance is what a composition cannot be—simultaneously a product and process. The simultaneity derives from the visual dimension of the theater. What we see exists; as we see it, it is happening. There is no lag between creation, manifestation, and perception.

Whenever the language of *Not and Now* encounters physical reality, language comes off as less powerful than that which can be seen. For example, in a meditation on money we learn that money is an object. It exists, occupies space. "Money is there" (432). Language can help us to know that money exists by pointing to it, by naming it. "Money is money" (432). But language does not have the power of altering or controlling the fact of money's existence in the objective world (or in the play world, for that matter). "There is no use saying money is not so. / It is" (431). Spoken language, in fact, can be a barrier to knowledge rather than a gateway, since it can so easily be the source of confusion. "They do not know oh no because of know and no." By contrast, "It is easy to see what is seen" (433). For example, "the difference between pale green and white" is the subject of a long meditation which concludes "and nobody that is not one of them who was looking like the one that one was looking like looked at anything that was pale green when they were looking at anything that was white. And when they did this what were they seeing. Could anybody who looked like anyone see pale green when they were looking at white" (437). The characters may call white pale green, but they can see only one color, the true color.

Furthermore, that which we see is always present, and as long as we see it, it continues to occupy the present. The characters in *Not and Now* would not be part of the past were it not for the language that connects them to people who cannot actually be present during a performance. As Stein herself declares, "as they [the characters] are looked at they are" (433). The minute we report our perception, that perception is past. Language does not have the immediacy of the objective world.

The last scene of *Not and Now* is composed of two long, almost unpunctuated paragraphs and an intervening paragraph of one short sentence. In the scene we are told, as Stein writes in her last line, "what was happening." The scene begins in the present and moves through the past progressive to the simple past, which is exactly what happens to action as it is told. Although the written text is a "telling," the scene, if performed, would actually take place in silence because the characters only look, see, and are seen. They do not speak. Since the text is a narration in past tense, it cannot coincide with an activity occurring on the stage in the present. Even if the narration were to be read as the scene proceeded, the tense of its verbs would indicate it was telling about an action that had already happened, not one that is happening as the narrative is being read. Language, this play tells us, is always a re-port, re-prise, re-sponse, or re-creation. It is never the thing itself; rather, it looks back at the thing. Once we begin "telling" what is seen (or thought or experienced), we are moving away from that thing:

> Picasso he does not know that he does look like Picasso. . . . The one who looks like Dashiell Hammett does not mean anything when he is saying anything and that thing because he never says anything does mean to say that day after day any day before any day which is what he does not say *he does not know that he looks like Dashiell Hammett and there is of course no one to tell him so* because no one can know that there is one who looks like him that is to say he does look like him . . . as everybody looks at him but nobody looks at him and so nobody sees him he looking as he is looking which is that he looks like him he is the one who looks like Dashiell Hammett and that is so and *nobody could say no if they were looking at him . . . he is that one.* (438) (emphasis added)

Not and Now can end either with a narration of what *was* happening or as a wordless *tableau vivant* in which something *is* happening. Stein is unable in this play to synchronize the language of her play and its performance. Even language used playfully to duplicate the only reality it could ever hope to duplicate, the mind's play, seems in this play dead and almost beside the point in performance, that perfect imaginative occupation of the present. The not and the now in *Not and Now* cannot be merged. The written play is a record of what is "not," no matter how closely it had registered the "now" of its composition. The "now" of performance demonstrates that the moment of the writing and the moment written about can only pretend to take place during performance.

In previous plays, Stein had created texts that could coexist with the other elements of performance, holding their own on the stage. In *Not and Now*, she seems to withdraw her text from that arena. The text is a narration of something past. As for the moment of performance, it is a textual void in which actors exist and are seen. No one acts; nothing happens; no one speaks. Stein had written a play that cannot play in the theater.

Listen to Me, the other play Stein wrote in 1936, is more successful than *Not and Now* at making peace between language and the other elements of performance. As I have already mentioned, it bears a formal resemblance to *Four Saints*. The text is a mixture of authorial commentary and ascribed speeches. It has the same tentative, improvised quality as *Four Saints*.

As she was in *Four Saints*, Stein, the writer, is on stage with her characters in *Listen to Me*. She begins the play by asserting her control as creator and leader of the play. *Listen to Me* she calls it, and "listen to me" she commands at intervals. She dictates the rules under which the game is to be played. The first of these is that there is to be no number five in her play, and the second, that there are to be no polysyllables. Since she is the writer, the play ought to take shape according to these rules. However, the players in *Listen to Me* prove to be more recalcitrant than the saints of *Four Saints*, and the leader loses control of the game. In *Listen to Me* Stein plays with the fact that her play cannot control the physical world which it creates. There is an inevitable collision between Stein's conception and its projected enactment—a collision that she engineers almost as though she wanted to look at it and think about it.

Stein's first rule is challenged immediately. Although she announces that the play will have three characters, she soon changes her mind. "A chorus of three characters and then a chorus of four characters but the characters that are the three characters are not the same characters as the characters that are the four characters."[13] Now Stein has seven characters in a play which is not supposed to have a number five. Since there cannot be a number five, Stein divides her seven into three and four, as though by that expedient the number five can be avoided. "There are never five characters in listen to me. . . . Three four seven characters yes because seven is seven. / How sweet of seven to be seven" (388).

Think, though, what will happen when the individual characters come alive and begin to speak. If each one of seven has a number, then there will be a number five. Stein solves the problem temporarily by using indirect discourse, preventing the characters from speaking and from occupying perceptual space. They are still only concepts in Stein's mind and can be referred to, if she wishes, without using the number five.

She imagines them spatially on a number line and identifies them by position so that number seven is called the last, and number six, the next to the last. Number five is not fifth then, but third from the end. The fifth number from the end is not number five but number three. Thus Stein avoids having a number five. Since the characters do not speak, there is no fifth character unless Stein tells us there is. When number five speaks, Stein writes: "The third from the last now speaks which is not the same as is now speaking. But is it. He says: I am forty now it is funny isn't it. I am forty now and that is funny." Then number three, who is fifth, but not five, is reported to have spoken: "The fifth one from the end one said. What is a genius she said" (389).

In spite of Stein's machinations, the existence of number five cannot be avoided forever. This play of Stein's is a play, and the characters will move and speak (unless she keeps the play forever in past tense and indirect discourse as she does in *Not and Now*). As soon as the characters are activated they will violate Stein's rule. (Of course, Stein could have avoided the whole dilemma by adhering to her original specification, that there be only three characters in *Listen to Me*. It seems, however, that she wishes to test her medium by posing such problems for it.) Stein must confront her characters. "And she lay down on a sofa. All five characters rushed up. But there are not five not even alive" (390). Once we, and she, see five characters rushing up, once, that is, that the action moves from the narrative past tense to the live present, there will be five characters. The same thing will happen when the five begin talking directly to us, as Stein shortly notes: "So then as often as any one all the characters are talking. To talk is very pleasant when it looks like writing. That is what three said when they were five. But there are never five" (391). When number three was fifth, and number five third, talking looked like writing, there was no number five, and everything was "very pleasant." However, in the face of objective reality, it is impossible for Stein to maintain her play rule. In Act 2, Stein calls for three characters and two characters to enter. Although she allows the first three to speak, the five stand before us to be counted. Stubbornly Stein announces, "Three and two do not make five because five is a number that they do not use therefore three and two make six." Such a rule violates logic, an acceptable violation when we are dealing with an imaginary world where Stein can create her own logic which we must accept as truth.

However, when the imagination tries to create an extralinguistic reality, through description or evocation, it must abide by certain standards. The extralinguistic world possesses qualities which the mind cannot alter.

Thus, on the next page of the play, "very quietly, five enter" (394). Stein has the first, second, and third characters speak individually, then has all the characters speak together, and finally writes, "Suddenly in the midst of all this silence somebody begins talking" (394). In fact, there has not been silence over all. Many of the characters have been speaking. However, one person has been silent—namely, the fifth character. Now number five begins talking. His first words: "I am there." Incontrovertible truth. Stein's manipulation notwithstanding, five exists.

Then begins an ongoing dialogue between Stein and her characters in which the characters try to force their autonomous physical existence on Stein. She resists:

> Listen to me does anybody know for certain how many characters there are.
> First character. I can count them.
> Second character. Count them.
> Third character. I count them
> Fourth character. There is no use counting them
> Fifth character. What you need to do is to count them
>> Curtain. [Stein tries to end the play, remove that fifth character from our sight.]
> First character. I know I am
> Second character. Who told you
> Third character. What did they tell you
> Fourth character. If they told you did you know or did you only know that they told you so.
> Fifth character. The best thing to do is to know the first character by looking.
> All together. Which is the first character.
> All together. The first character. (395–396)

In the 1923 play, *A List*, characters and actors were at the mercy of language and, thus, at the mercy of the playwright. Here, language seems superfluous—not a key to ultimate knowledge but just a key to itself. "If they told you did you know or did you only know that they told you so." Stein's play seems to tell us that in the theater what we see is what we know. What we hear is only what we hear. Whereas *A*

List asserts the primacy of language, *Listen to Me* asserts the primacy of action and actor.

An even more severe test of language is presented by the second rule of play in *Listen to Me*—that the play be composed entirely of monosyllables. Stein should have had little trouble tailoring her writing to such self-imposed demands. Whatever is written has only to correspond to concepts generated by the mind of Gertrude Stein. In a play, however, whatever is written must create a reality to be perceived and must correspond to the reality it has set in motion. For example, if Stein's play has created a confusion, that confusion exists, in spite of the fact that the name for it has more than one syllable. "This sounds like a confusion but confusion is more than two syllables" (398). Stein could search for a monosyllabic synonym, or she could refuse to name what she has created, but her language rule and her language game cannot modify or eliminate the confusion which an audience might perceive. The text, once realized and made public, has activated autonomous events, and must abide by rules other than those governing its composition. In *Listen to Me*, for instance, Stein notes that "curtain" has two syllables. She therefore maintains that there can be no curtain in the play. No curtain—no end. Without an end, *Listen to Me* becomes an eternal present. That would, of course, please Stein. She makes much of the timelessness of her play. "No one literally no one must remember anything" (391). Why not? Because, "after a quiet moment there is no quiet moment . . . after or before. . . . Why not . . . Because there is no after or before" (410). If there is no after or before, there is no temporal order. "Sunday is Sunday afternoon but it does not come after Saturday or before Monday" (409). The immediate present is therefore not a departure from the past nor a preparation for the future. There is no "suddenly" in *Listen to Me* (405).

However pleasant for her to contemplate, Stein's ideal of temporal suspension, a play without a curtain, is impossible to maintain. The play must end. The last act is a fact, and even in *Listen to Me*, the curtain will come. If Stein needed to have a sense of an unlimited time span in order to express her mind (which does not go on but stays within), then a play would have been a disappointment to her. No matter what else a play is or does, it must set a temporal limit on the play of the mind, because in the theater, and in the theater alone, play time corresponds to audience time. The audience, and the actors for that matter, cannot play forever.

Stein had always resisted endings, and certainly never planned on them, preferring to let them take her by surprise. In *Everybody's Autobiography* she explains how she feels about endings:

There was of course science and evolution [in the nineteenth century] and there were of course the fact that stars were worlds and that space had no limitation and still if civilizations always came to be dead of course they had to come to be dead since the earth had no more size than it had how could other civilizations come if those that were did not come to be dead . . . I had always been afraid always would be afraid but after all was that what it was to be not refusing to be dead although after all every one was refusing to be dead. . . . I can remember being very excited when I first read the Old Testament to see that they never spoke of a future life, there was a God there was eternity but there was no future life and I found how naturally that worried me.[14]

On the one hand, death, the ultimate end, is a worry, but on the other hand, if life never ended, the earth would soon be covered over with people, as it is in *Listen to Me*. Stein implies elsewhere in *Everybody's Autobiography* that the genius is immune to the winds of change which buffet the rest of us. Luckily Stein was, by her own account, a genius. Sweet William, the wandering "hero" of *Listen to Me*, is also a genius, and thereby escapes, it seems, the rule of those temporal laws by which normal people are governed. Stein describes Sweet William as follows:

> Sweet William prepared verdure.
> Sweet William prepared pools.
> Verdure two syllables
> Pools one
> Sweet William prepared what he had.
> Had one syllable
> He one syllable
> What one syllable
> Prepared. Three Syllables
> Sweet William prepared verdure and fountains and he admired what he did.
> Sweet William continued to prepare verdure and fountains and continued to admire what he did. (399)

The genius continues his or her activities even if they violate rules. Nevertheless, there is one limit beyond which Sweet William cannot proceed. At the end of the play "Sweet William is nowhere to be seen." As the curtain must come to the play, the end must come to Sweet William. However, Sweet William has involved himself with activities of renewal: the recurrent green of spring, the fountain welling from its source, the pools that hold the water from earth and sky in an eternal circle. Like the flower for which he is named, Sweet William's genius will not disappear when its physical incarnation, its flower, dies. It will come again in the next flowering. Sweet William will continue to admire his work because his work will always continue.

The incarnation of Stein's genius is her writing. She must record the play of the mind in order to know what she knows. More importantly, she must make that record public in order for the play to survive the player. It is only by seeing the play that we know the player. It is only through repetition, ritualization, memory, and history that the mind survives the body, that *Listen to Me* survives Gertrude Stein. She writes in *Everybody's Autobiography*:

Whenever I write a play it is a play because it is a thing I do not see but it is a thing somebody can see that is what makes a play to me. When I see a thing it is not a play to me because the minute I see it it ceases to be a play for me, but when I write something that somebody else can see then it is a play for me . . . when I write a play then it is something that is inside of me but if I could see it then it would not be.[15]

A play for Gertrude Stein is anything she cannot see; it is whatever is in her mind. But Gertrude Stein's play cannot be our play unless we can see it. When she relinquishes the play, "it ceases." However, by accepting the cessation of her own play, she creates the possibility of the perpetual renewal of the play we see.

It is because *Listen to Me* can begin again that the curtain can finally come. The play ends with these lines:

Acts
Curtain
Characters
Characters
Curtain
Acts
There is no one and one
Nobody has met anyone.
        Curtain Can Come.
        Curtain (421)

The first six lines demonstrate that this and every play is a circle which ends only to begin again in its next enactment. As endings give way to new beginnings, absence (no one, nobody) gives way to presence (one, anyone). Because this is so, "Curtain can come," and it does.

Chapter 4

Acts, Characters, Curtain: The Last Plays, 1938 to 1946

I

The plays Gertrude Stein wrote between 1938 and her death in 1946 are more conventional than any she had written in previous decades.[1] For example, the two plays I will be considering in this chapter, *Doctor Faustus Lights the Lights* (1938) and *The Mother of Us All* (1945), have characters that are coherently portrayed through speech and action. They have plots in which events unfold sequentially and which draw characters into internal and external conflict and toward the resolution of conflict. These plays do not resist enactment; rather, they provide actors with an abundance of performance "opportunities." They do not defy interpretation; on the contrary, they facilitate it by ample use of conventional symbolism, historical and literary allusions, and overt thematic content.

Nonetheless, despite their relative conventionality, *Doctor Faustus* and *The Mother of Us All* retain a number of the techniques and characteristics that marked the earlier plays. In both plays, however, Stein accommodates her experimentation to theatrical necessity as she never had before, and thus, both "play" well in the theater. So, for example, although the language in both plays is stylized and repetitive and sound is at least as important as sense in many of the speeches, neither play exhibits the extreme fragmentation and the militant nonreferentiality of earlier plays. And similarly, although both plays violate dramatic convention by mixing dramatic discourse with narrative and indirect discourse, they abide by the more fundamental conventions of plot and characterization.

Stein's integration of experimentation and conventionality in her plays mirrors a similar integration taking place in her other writing. Like any writer, Stein had always wanted readers, but she had almost never been willing to alter her style in order to attract them. In the early thirties, she decided, as she wrote to Carl Van Vechten, that "the time has come to reach the audience that is there."[2] One of her methods for reaching an audience was to publish herself. She and Toklas started their own publishing company, The Plain Edition, which eventually published five books by Stein. However, publishing the books did not guarantee that there would be an audience for them. In a different and more successful effort to reach an audience, Stein began to work increasingly in public modes: autobiography, lecture, journalism. In these "public" works, communication was as important a goal as experimentation because in them Stein sought to explain her life and her poetics. Nonetheless, Stein was unhappy with publishers who were eager to bring out her public books like *The Autobiography of Alice B. Toklas* and *Lectures in America* but were unwilling to publish her less accessible, experimental writing. In a letter to her agent, William Aspenwall Bradley, she complained of this double standard:

He [Harcourt] should realize that my reputation is and was made by the kind of book that Grant [*Four in America*] is and that a certain proportion of them should be printed by him before he does another of the kind he likes which will be the volume of essays or lectures which I am doing for the lecture series. Do try to make him see that what he calls open and public books are really illustrations for the other books, and that illustrations should accompany what they illustrate.[3]

In writing plays, Stein had always been wary of the public performance that would eventually befall the text, and she had always valorized the written text over its public enactment. In the last years of her life, however, plays joined autobiographies, lectures, and journalism as modes through which she could record, represent, and explain her life, and therefore, the text had to accommodate the performance through which it would be communicated to the public, and experimentation had to give way to accessibility. In a sense, these plays, like other works of the late thirties and the forties, were "illustrated" works in which the conventional illustration accompanied the experimental text.

The most notable difference between the earlier, more experimental plays and the two late plays I will be discussing here is the absence of the writer and the writing process from the later plays. *Doctor Faustus* and *The Mother of Us All* are not about "the process and materials of their own construction" as earlier plays had been. They do not dramatize the conflict between the written text and the performance as earlier plays had done. They are not metadramas in the same sense that earlier plays had been.

Nonetheless, insofar as both plays are concerned with people who transform their private selves into public characters, stepping into the center-stage spotlight, as it were, and acting a public role that requires they set aside certain private weaknesses and desires, then these plays, too, are metadramas. The figures who undergo this process and transformation are Marguerite in *Doctor Faustus* and Susan B. Anthony in *The Mother of Us All*; both characters are somewhat autobiographical surrogates for the playwright herself.

The private self that must be abandoned is the feminine side of these characters; the public self is the masculine side, its characteristics derived from male role models (who are also characters in these plays). Marguerite and Susan B. Anthony must develop these masculine qualities if they are to succeed at playing their roles in public life. *Doctor Faustus* and *The Mother of Us All*, then, are also unique among Stein's plays in having overtly feminist thematic content. Some of Stein's earliest work, *Fernhurst, Three Lives, Two*, and part of *The Making of Americans*, all of which predated her first play by many years, had dealt with women and women's lives from a feminist perspective. The more experimental Stein's writing became, however, the less it was "about" female experience. Marianne DeKoven suggests that this was "a shift of the rebellious impulse . . . to the structure of language itself," a transferal of antipatriarchal sentiment from content to form.[4] Although I do not characterize Stein's experimentation as antipatriarchal, I do agree with DeKoven that "specifically female material, and perhaps feminist intention" begin to resurface in Stein's later writing.[5] In Stein's writing for the theater, the shift away from experimentation and back to antipatriarchal content occurred in the last decade of her life, and specifically in the two plays I will be discussing here.

Although seven years separate their composition, *Doctor Faustus* and *The Mother of Us All* function as companion pieces. Both represent crises in a woman's life: *Doctor Faustus* represents the moment of sexual initiation and a girl's struggle against her biological destiny; *The Mother of Us All* dramatizes a woman's efforts to define herself and to participate as an equal in a man's world. Both plays draw on male-generated texts (the Faust myth and American history) to tell antipatriarchal stories. They are Gertrude Stein's revisions of those texts to make them tell her story, to reenact her renunciation of procreation in favor of creation and her definition of herself as a peer of Picasso and Joyce, and co-creator with them of modernism.

II

When Gertrude Stein wrote *Doctor Faustus Lights the Lights*, she expected Gerald Berners to set it to music. He had already scored her play, *A Bouquet. Their Wills*, as a ballet called *A Wedding Bouquet* for Sadlers Wells. Whether Stein or Berners chose the subject of their second "collaboration" is not entirely clear. Stein had stayed with Berners in London for the premiere of *A Wedding Bouquet* in April 1937, and both Carl Van Vechten, in his introduction to *Last Operas and Plays*, and Richard Bridgman, in *Gertrude Stein in Pieces*, refer to Berners as having commissioned the work. However, the Berners/Stein correspondence does not indicate that Stein began *Doctor Faustus* at Berners' request. In an explanatory note to a letter from Berners to Stein, in which Berners acknowledges receipt of the completed manuscript, Donald Gallup writes that "Lord Berners had come to Paris, and Gertrude Stein had shown him part of a new opera, 'Dr. Faustus Lights the Lights,' which she had just begun to write."[6] Following this visit, in a letter from England, Berners asks Stein to send him "the first act of Doctor Faustus" and adds, "I was very thrilled by what you showed me and read to me—and I want to have it by me and as soon as I've finished my present business I'll start on it."[7] If the idea for the opera was Berners's, clearly he was not ready to work on it, and in fact, he never did write the music for it. In December 1939, he wrote to Stein that "all inspirational sources seem to have dried up: I can't write a note of music or do any kind of creative work whatever and it's not for want of trying and I don't believe I shall be able to as long as this war lasts."[8]

Whether Stein herself had chosen the subject of the new opera, or whether it had evolved, as had that of *Four Saints*, from conversations with the composer, Stein was evidently more amenable to using a "historical" subject in 1938 than she had been in 1927 when she wrote *Four Saints*. In *Four Saints* historical fact and saintly lore are subsidiary to Stein's metatextual explorations. In *Doctor Faustus Lights the Lights*, on the other hand, the history of Doctor Faustus is part of the drama, and metatextual content is replaced by feminist content.

In a postcard to Carl Van Vechten, Stein writes that she has just finished *Doctor Faustus*. "The theology and the drama will I hope be to you[r] likeing."[9] She was certainly not the first writer to use the Faust legend to express a "theology." The story of a man who sells his soul to the devil in exchange for magical powers appears in the folklore of almost all countries. The Western version of this legend is actually based on a historical figure, Georg Helmstetter, born in Germany circa 1466, who later assumed the Latin name Faustus. He was a philosopher and an astrologer, trained at Heidelberg, but his chief fame came from his soothsaying and necromancy, and his practice of other magic arts. He became a legendary figure almost immediately after his death (some time before 1539), and his story was recorded and circulated to warn against wicked and impure practices and against pacts with ungodly powers. Eventually, the Faust figure became associated with intellectual curiosity; his desire for knowledge and power became his chief sin, the "original" sin which had led to his consorting with the devil in the first place. In her adaptation of the story, Stein demonstrates her familiarity with the details and variations of the legend and with the uses other writers had made of it.[10]

Stein's Doctor Faustus, like those before him, has traded his soul for knowledge that will allow him to transcend human limitations, especially to elude death and darkness and to enjoy perpetual life and light. In Stein's play Mephistopheles, or Mephisto as she most often calls him, has shown Doctor Faustus how to invent the electric light, and as a consequence of his invention, Faustus lives in a world (and wanders on a stage) that is permanently incandescent. With an unending light source, Faustus has an endless day, and by extension, endless life. Like a plant growing under artificial light, he knows no seasons. Unless he is uprooted, he need never know death.

As a character, Stein's Doctor Faustus has much in common with Marlowe's Faustus, whose name he bears. Marlowe's drama is a tragedy of despair; his Faustus loses faith, not only in God's capacity for forgiveness, but also in the very knowledge for which he has made his bargain with the devil. Stein's Faustus, too, comes to realize the folly of his overreaching desires. He believes that his pact with the devil was unnecessary since, as he realizes too late, he could have invented electric light on his own if he had taken his time. He laments his mistake:

> I am Doctor Faustus who knows everything can do everything and you [the devil] say it was through you but not at all, if I had not been in a hurry and if I had taken my time I would have known how to make white electric light . . . and what did I do I saw you miserable devil I saw you and I was deceived and I believed miserable devil I thought I needed you.[11]

It was Faustus's impatience, not his impotence, which led him to call on Mephisto. He understands that he has lost his soul in exchange for a power that was his to begin with.

Moreover, the power he sought—the power over the source of light, and thus over time—has proved an unwelcome burden and further cause for despair. He has begun to weary of eternal wakefulness in an eternally well-lit present. His invention frustrates his organic need for dark, for sleep, and for death. Accordingly, when we first meet him, he appears "at the door of his room, with his arms up at the door lintel looking out, behind him a blaze of electric light" (89). His position demonstrates his rejection of the infinite light source he has invented. With his back to the light and his face in shadow, he has already taken the first step of his journey from light, a journey that will end when he "sinks into the darkness" at the play's conclusion (118).

He now welcomes darkness and death because he has learned that his prized freedom from death is an exclusion from life as well, from that natural cycle manifest in the sun's alternate presence and absence, and in the moon's repeated growth and diminution. Since making his compact with Mephisto to eradicate darkness, Doctor Faustus has come to realize that the dark gives meaning to the light, the negative to the positive. As he says, "I keep on having so much light that light is not bright" (89). He also realizes that the perpetual present for which he has bargained has deprived him of hope, which requires a future, and memory, which requires a past. He rails against his condition:

> There is no snake to grind under one's heel, there is no hope there is no death there is no life there is no breath, there just is every day all day and when there is no day there is no day. . . .
>
> . . . everything is always now and now and now . . . I begin to know . . . that light however bright will never be other than light, and any light is just a light and now there is nothing more either by day or by night but just a light. (90)

As Doctor Faustus now understands, life and death are linked in an unbreakable circle of existence, cessation, and renewal, like the snake with its tail in its mouth, representing both destruction and regeneration, and so a fitting symbol of the continuity of life. In the world of Doctor Faustus's invention there is "no snake to grind under one's heel." To crush the serpent's head is to sow his teeth, the seeds of future generations. To live is to participate in the process of generation, and death is a necessary stage in that process. For Doctor Faustus, "there is," as he puts it, "no death, there is no life."

Therefore, Faustus spends his entire time on stage looking for death at any cost, even at the cost of eternal damnation. He will gladly go to hell rather than continue as master of the lights in his illuminated hell on earth. Ironically, he does not understand that Mephisto can assist him to achieve this goal, just as he had formerly misinterpreted the part Mephisto played in the invention of "white electric light." Like Marlowe's hero, Stein's Doctor Faustus has an imperfect understanding of the devil and his powers.

Mephisto's purpose in the play is to conduct Faustus on the journey from life to death. Familiar with the dark underworld, he can lead Faustus to it. He has the power to engulf the stage in darkness. But because Mephisto gave Faustus eternal life and light, Faustus cannot recognize him as the source of death and the Prince of Darkness. He sees him only as the source and custodian of the accursed light. Thus, Faustus unknowingly spurns his dark deliverer when he kicks Mephisto off the stage, shouting after him, "Get out of here devil just you go to hell" (91). Unwittingly, in his curse Faustus has identified Mephisto's origin and destination; however, he remains oblivious to the literal truth behind the metaphorical curse. When Mephisto leaves Faustus alone, the stage lights become brighter than ever before. The devil's dimming presence was an unmistakable sign of his dark powers. Yet, again, Faustus seems unaware of the import of the phenomenon he is witnessing.

Similarly, Faustus misunderstands the role of the dog that enters after Faustus has kicked Mephisto off the stage. The dog has the gift of speech. His most common expression is "thank you." In its polite and gentle tones, the dog's speech resembles Mephisto's. (As in Marlowe's play, the devil here speaks like a patient parent or a polite helpmeet, while Doctor Faustus whines like a demanding and petulant child.) The devil traditionally assumes the form of a dog, and the possibility that the dog is a manifestation of the devil is further reinforced by the dog's power over the stage lights.

When the dog enters and says his first "thank you," one of the lights goes out. As Faustus dances with the dog, the "electric lights come and go" and get "pale" (92). But Faustus does not recognize the dog's power nor does he make any connection between the dog and the devil. Again, Faustus unknowingly pushes another potential "rescuer" away from him. He wishes only to be left alone:

Let me alone
Oh let me alone
Dog and boy let me alone oh let me alone
Leave me alone
Let me be alone
little boy and dog
let let me alone (93)

When at the end of the play, Doctor Faustus recognizes that Mephisto is the one person who can assist him in going to hell, he accepts his intercession without hesitation:

Faustus
Well then how dear devil how how can I who have no soul I sold it for a light how can I be I again alright and go to hell.
   Mephisto
Commit a sin
   Faustus
What sin, how can I without a soul commit a sin.
   Mephisto
Kill anything
   Faustus
Kill
   Mephisto
Yes kill something oh yes kill anything. (116)

Faustus arranges the murder of the dog and his boy companion. They are bitten and poisoned by a viper (another manifestation of the devil). Having killed something on the devil's instructions, Faustus is himself now able to die. Because he dies in darkness and sin, unrepentant and unredeemed, he will go to hell.

The disappointing career of Stein's Doctor Faustus and its dark end remind one of the pessimism of Marlowe's play. Despite playful and comic elements (again reminiscent of Marlowe's combination of the serious and the comic), we do not find in Stein's representation of the Faust legend the optimism of Goethe's version of Faust's life of error and of his ultimate redemption. Yet in one important respect, Stein's play is more akin to Goethe's than to Marlowe's and that is in the addition of a female character to the story. As Goethe introduced Margarete (Gretchen) to the Faust legend, Stein creates a character called Marguerite Ida and Helena Annabel (two compound names, one character). Though she bears the name Helena, she does not resemble in the least Helen of Troy who represents female sexual power and destructiveness in both Marlowe and Goethe. Rather, she is Stein's version of the Margarete/Gretchen figure in Goethe.[12]

In an essay on the role of women in the Faust story, Nancy Kaiser writes, "We might conclude [from the texts Kaiser examines and the examples she gives] that there is a cultural injunction which discourages women's appropriation of Faust."[13] Stein defies this cultural injunction not only by appropriating Faust, but also by altering significantly the role of the woman in the story.

By creating a hero closer to Marlowe's Faustus than to Goethe's

Faust, Stein skews the balance between male and female which Goethe established through the pairing of Margarete and Faust. Goethe's Faust is the archetypal questing male hero. In her essay *"Faust*: The Tragedy Reexamined,"* Margaret Guenther describes the Faustian man as "active, questing, and free. The strictures of society do not bind him, for—with divine approval—all experience is open to him and all activity sanctioned. He is the ultimate consumer, moving through time, space, and human lives, picking up and discarding at will."[14] In Guenther's view the "necessary counterbalance" to this hero is the "suffering heroine" and that is the role played by Margarete in Part 1 of Goethe's drama. Faust "has achieved moral and intellectual clarity at the cost of human suffering, epitomized in the figure of Margarete."[15] Marlowe's Faustus is a less exalted, more debased hero than Goethe's Faust. As A. N. Okerlund writes, Marlowe's play is concerned with "rational man suborning his logical being in the quest for immortality."[16] Marlowe's Faustus abuses reason and language. He chooses "a life of stasis where knowledge was delivered to him by Mephostophilis, rather than a life [of] vitality where he, himself, would search for and discover truth."[17] By pairing Marguerite with such a hero, Stein reverses the relationship between the male and female figures. Since the male is passive and suffering, the female can be active and questing. The very structure and focus of the drama reflect this reversal.

Despite its title, *Doctor Faustus Lights the Lights* begins when the bulk of Faustus's story is already over. Like the blind Faust in the second part of Goethe's play, Stein's Doctor Faustus is simply waiting to die. His is the drama of reconciliation in which he must deal with consequences of actions already taken. Because he repeatedly retreats and withdraws from action and thrusts other actors from him, he almost seems extraneous to the drama. It occurs around him but does not engage him. He keeps looking for a way out of it. Marguerite, on the other hand, is central to the drama. She is the focus of conflict since hers is not a story of reconciliation but of initiation. She must repeatedly take action and make choices. In the course of the play, she seems to recapitulate struggles we imagine Doctor Faustus to have had prior to the time of the drama, but, and this is key to understanding Stein's "theology," Marguerite's experience will not, in fact, recapitulate Doctor Faustus's since she is a female, and the history of her development must necessarily recapitulate a female, not a male phylogeny. What then is the history of the female which Marguerite's experience exemplifies and how does it differ from Doctor Faustus's?

For Doctor Faustus, the source of destruction was his overreaching intellectual ambition. Mephisto tempted him with knowledge and with power over natural forces. For Marguerite, the danger lies in her sexuality. Mephisto tempts her with courtship and with the safety from threatening forces to be found in the arms of a male other.

When first we see Marguerite, she stands on the verge of a dark and wild wood; she is confused and frightened:

> I wish, (she whispered) I knew why woods are wild why animals are wild why I am I, why I can cry, I wish I wish I knew, I wish oh how I wish I knew. Once I am in I will never be through the woods are there and I am here and am I here or am I there, oh where oh where is here oh where oh where is there and animals wild animals are everywhere. (95)

In this fairy-tale setting, the childlike Marguerite is about to become a woman. Having entered the woods, she is bitten by a serpent that emerges from the undergrowth. The sexual significance of the episode is unmistakable:

> Does it hurt she says and then she says no not really and she says was it a viper and she says how can I tell I never saw one before but is it she says and she stands up again and sits down and pulls down her stocking and says well it was not a bee not a busy bee no not, nor a mosquito. (96–97)

It was indeed the phallic viper, not the female bee or the female mosquito, that violated Marguerite.

Marguerite's encounter has more than sexual significance, however, as the appearance on the stage of "a country woman with a sickle" reminds us. Like the woman with the sickle, the serpent—or viper, as Marguerite calls it—symbolizes not only sexuality but also fertility and death. Not only has Marguerite been sexually initiated, she has also been drawn more fully into life/death processes. However, like Doctor Faustus before her, Marguerite has no intention of succumbing to death. The country woman brings her to Doctor Faustus, whom she is certain "can make it all well" (99). At first Faustus refuses. Marguerite begs: "A viper has had his bite and I I will die but you you cannot die you have sold your soul but I I have mine and a viper has come and he has bitten me and see see how the poison works see see how I must die" (101). Finally, with a few words Faustus works a magical cure and saves her life: "Enough said. You are not dead. Enough said" (103).

After her rescue by Doctor Faustus, Marguerite appears in a halo of candlelight, holding an artificial viper. "This is not a viper. This is what is like a viper," the chorus sings (105). Like an enthroned deity, the apotheosis of the female, Marguerite holds court with her back to the sun. The people flock to see her:

> They come from everywhere
> By land by sea by air
> They come from everywhere
> To look at her there.
> See how she sits
> See how she eats
> See how she lights,
> The candlelights.
> See how the viper there,
> Cannot hurt her.
>
> . . .
>
> Nothing can touch her,
>
> . . .
>
> Nothing can lose her,
>
> . . .
>
> And she sits
> With her back to the sun
> One sun
> And she is one (106–107)

For the sun Marguerite has substituted candles; for the real viper, an amulet; for sexual union, singularity; for nature, art. These substitutions have empowered her. She is one, like the sun. And here the pun suggests that she is not like a daughter, but like a son, male in her authority, male in her singularity. All of this she has accomplished without selling her soul to the devil.

It is at this point that the devil begins to work on Marguerite (though, in fact he has already made a tentative beginning as the viper in the undergrowth). The temptation of Marguerite, unlike that of Doctor Faustus, occurs after her elevation to a position of power, immune from natural forces. As she sits in her singular glory, "a man from over the seas" approaches her and courts her with sweet endearments:

> Pretty pretty dear
> She is all my love and always here
> And I am hers and she is mine
> And I love her all the time
> Pretty pretty pretty dear. (107)

Although Marguerite weakens—once dropping the viper amulet, her artificial phallus, once fainting, a stereotypically feminine response to danger—she does not yield because she senses that the man from over the seas is not what he appears to be: "You are as you are not" (108). At first, Marguerite suspects the man to be Doctor Faustus in disguise. "Is it you Doctor Faustus is it you, tell me man from over the sea are you he." Marguerite puzzles over the man's duplicity.

> No one is one when there are two, look behind you look behind you you are not one you are two.
> She faints.
> And indeed behind the man of the seas is Mephistopheles. (108)

The courtly man who speaks of love is actually a front man for Mephisto. A boy and girl who accompany Mephisto begin to call the man from over the seas Mr. Viper. The viper in the woods, the loving man, and Mephisto are conflated, all three agents of destruction, all three envoys of the devil.

Mephisto is not immediately successful in his seduction and destruction of Marguerite. She still has the power of the light, power that comes from being one like the sun. She has supplanted Faustus. Since he has wanted to give up his power throughout the play, he welcomes her ascension; it signals his release. He announces: "If she can turn night into day then I can go to hell . . . if she can turn night into day as they say then I am not the only one . . . so Marguerite Ida and Helena Annabel listen well you cannot but I I can go to hell. Come on every one never again will I be alone" (113).

Before Mephisto will allow Doctor Faustus to die, he sets him a final task—to seduce Marguerite and to take her to hell with him. Mephisto transforms Doctor Faustus into a young man. Despite his rejuvenation, he is unsuccessful in his wooing because he reveals to her his true intention. Unfortunately for Marguerite, the danger she perceives in Doctor Faustus's seduction forces her back fainting into the arms of the man from over the seas, who sings, "Pretty pretty pretty dear I am he and she is she and we are we, pretty pretty dear I am here yes I am here pretty pretty pretty dear" (118). The grammar of the song makes plain what is happening to Marguerite: the male first-person singular, "I am he," absorbs the female third-person singular, "she is she," into a male-generated first-person plural, "we are we." She no longer exists, but he is still the speaking subject.

With Marguerite absorbed, as it were, by the man from over the seas, the light is out, the candle snuffed. The stage is entirely dark. The last voices we hear from somewhere on the darkened stage are those of the presexual little boy and little girl. They address the darkness: "Please Mr. Viper listen to me." There is no answer, but we can imagine Mr. Viper waiting in the darkness for the boy to grow to manhood and the girl to womanhood, when he can begin again the process which we have just witnessed in *Doctor Faustus Lights the Lights*.

III

Seven years after writing *Doctor Faustus*, Stein deals with the same issue again in *The Mother of Us All*. Again she dramatizes the conflict between a female's desire for power and authority and her sexual and emotional need to merge with a male other. Susan B. Anthony, the heroine of the play, resisted her biological destiny—never marrying, never having children—much like Gertrude Stein herself. Instead of becoming a natural mother, Susan B. Anthony is the metaphorical mother of us all.

That Stein identified to some extent with her heroine is clear from a bit of business at the beginning of the play. A character, designated as G. S. and making only one appearance, speaks twice about her father. First:

> My father's name was Daniel, Daniel and a bear, a bearded Daniel, not Daniel in the lion's den not Daniel, yes Daniel my father had a beard my father's name was Daniel.

And then:

> My father's name was Daniel he had a black beard he was not tall not at all tall, he had a black beard his name was Daniel.[18]

Stein's father was indeed named Daniel; he had a black beard, and he was, as she states, "not at all tall." Coincidentally, Susan B. Anthony's father was also named Daniel.

In her characterization of Anthony and in her dramatization of the suffragist's career, Stein draws heavily on historical record, even quoting from or alluding to Anthony's actual speeches.[19] For example, Susan B.'s first platform speech at the beginning of Act 2 is an excerpt from Susan B. Anthony's first public speech, delivered in 1849 at Canajoharie, New York, to the Daughters of Temperance. Anthony's speech reads: "Ladies! there is no Neutral position for us to assume. . . . If we say we love the Cause and then sit down at our ease, surely does our action speak the lie."[20] In her transposition from the historical record to the drama, Stein has changed not a word.

In this same scene Stein alludes to a speech made by Anthony at the very end of her career, thereby condensing a whole lifetime of public speaking into a brief theatrical scene. The later speech was made in 1896 to the Washington Convention of the National American Woman Suffrage Association. In it, Anthony chastised the membership for considering a resolution to repudiate *The Woman's Bible*, a "heretical" book published two months earlier by one of their own leaders, and Anthony's best friend, Elizabeth Cady Stanton. Anthony remonstrated:

To pass such a resolution is to set back the hands on the dial of reform. . . . We have all sorts of people in the Association and . . . a Christian has no more right on our platform than an atheist. When this platform is too narrow for people of all creeds and of no creeds to stand on, I myself shall not stand upon it.[21]

Instead of using Anthony's words, Stein abstracts the idea behind them, of the platform which embraces all points of view, and dramatizes it by having Susan, alone on a platform, addressed by one of the characters below:

Jo the Loiterer.   I have behind me a crowd, are we allowed.
Susan B.   A crowd is never allowed but each one of you can come in.
                   . . .
                   All the characters crowd in. (70)

The scene continues. Finally, "all the characters are crowding up on the platform" with Susan.

They Say.   Now we are all here there is nobody down there to hear, now if it is we're always like that there would be no reason why anybody should cry. (72)

With all of the characters upon the platform, no one, not even Susan B. Anthony has any reason to complain.

There are further parallels between Stein's character, Susan B., and the historical figure, Susan B. Anthony. Like the real figure who was raised a Quaker, Stein's character "was born a believer in peace" (58). Like the original, who was doubtful of her speaking abilities, Stein's Susan has to be encouraged by her companion to speak out and has to be instructed in the techniques of public speaking. Like the indefatigable suffragist who traveled and lectured without respite, Stein's heroine "began to follow, she began to follow herself. I am not tired said Susan. . . . This was the beginning. They began to travel not to travel you know but to go from one place to another place. In each place Susan B. said here I am I am here" (59).

Susan B. Anthony's lifelong sympathy for the working poor and her support of labor reform are represented in the play by the heroine's speech comparing rich to poor. "When they are rich . . . they do not listen and when they do they do not hear, and to be poor . . . is to be so poor they listen and listen and what they hear well what do they hear, they hear that they listen, they listen to hear, that is what it is to be poor" (69). The voiceless poor had a spokesperson in Susan B. Anthony.

The suffragist's campaign for the property rights of married women and her conviction that women must establish their independence apart from marriage (even to the point of retaining their maiden names) are also echoed in the play. The fictional Susan reminds her followers that

> even if they love them so, they are alone to live and die, they are alone to sink and swim they are alone to have what they own, to have no idea but that they are here, to struggle and thirst to do everything first, because until it is done there is no other one. (72)

Although Susan presides over the marriage of one of her followers, she questions the benefits of the institution. "What is marriage, is marriage protection or religion, is marriage renunciation or abundance, is marriage a stepping-stone or an end. What is marriage" (74).

As Susan B. Anthony fought for the enfranchisement of Blacks, so does Stein's heroine. Stein re-creates Anthony's disappointment over the ingratitude of male abolitionists and Blacks alike, who were not willing to extend the vote to women. To "a Negro Man" Susan says approximately what Susan B. Anthony said to Frederick Douglass at the 1869 convention of the American Equal Rights Association. "Negro man would you vote if you only can and not she. . . . I fought for you that you could vote would you vote if they would not let me." The "Negro man" responds much as Douglass did. "You bet" (67).

Susan also reproaches other male characters who represent those politicians who sought Susan B. Anthony's support during elections but, once elected, did not fulfill their promises to her:

Chorus.	Do come Susan B. Anthony do come . . . nobody can make them come the way you make them come . . . it is your duty, Susan B. Anthony . . . you know you know your duty. . . .
Susan B. Anthony.	I suppose I will be coming, is it because you flatter me, is it because if I do not come you will forget me and never vote my laws, you will never vote my laws even if I do come but if I do not come you will never vote my laws, come or not come it always comes to the same thing. . . .
All the Men.	Dear kind lady we count on you, and as we count on you so can you count on us.
Susan B. Anthony.	. . . I always hope that if I go that if I go and go and go, perhaps then you men will vote my laws but I know how well I know, a little this way a little that way you steal away, you steal a piece away you steal yourselves away, you do not intend to stay and vote my laws, and still when you call I go . . . this time you have to do more than promise, you must write it down that you will vote my laws, but no, you will pay no attention to what is written, well then swear by my hearth . . . swear after I work for you swear that you will vote my laws, but no, no oaths, no thoughts, no decisions, no intentions, no gratitude, no convictions, no nothing will make you pass my laws. (78–79)

Despite all of Anthony's work (including her arrest and prosecution for illegally voting in the presidential election of 1872), the right to vote was not extended to women in her lifetime.

Susan's chief adversary in Stein's play is Daniel Webster—another Daniel, another father. Webster makes the ideal antagonist for Anthony. Central to Anthony's argument for equal rights was her expressed conviction that women were as capable of the wise management of political and economic power as men. What better way for Stein to prove the justice of Anthony's claim than by choosing as her antagonist a man whose wisdom was not equal to his power. One of Webster's biographers describes him as a "great man flawed."[22] His greatness was more symbolic than real, his image a "product of studied effort" and a function of his considerable "dramatic talent."[23] Webster was ambitious, and as a result of his ambition, he played a "dominant national role as lawyer, orator, congressman, senator, secretary of state, and leader of two major parties,"[24] enjoying the kind of political power that was denied to women. But whether Webster deserved the power he held was another question entirely. As his biographer explains, "Although multitudes praised Webster, lavished him with attention, and probably read, wrote about, and listened to him more than any other leader of his time, the American people never came close to making him president. . . . A certain intimation of weakness, the perception of a marked streak of dependency within the magnificent carriage of the man, raised doubts even among his admirers."[25] The outer man was impressive; the inner less so.

Daniel Webster is also an ideal antagonist for Susan B. Anthony because he was her political and ideological opposite. His were the politics of expedience, hers of justice for all. He served the moneyed interests, she the powerless and poor. Webster was chronically dependent on the powerful creditors of the Bank of the United States, and his actions as senator and secretary of state were often determined by the wishes of the wealthy Massachusetts bankers who loaned him money and secured his election and appointment. Whether Webster's infamous 1850 speech in favor of the Fugitive Slave Law was prompted by such pecuniary considerations is not clear from the record. However, his morally objectionable willingness to placate Southern Whigs for his own political purposes was condemned on every side, most vigorously, of course, by the abolitionists. By contrast, on the issue of slavery, Susan B. Anthony was a fervent abolitionist.

Whereas Webster was said to drink too much, even in public, Anthony was a temperance leader. Whereas Webster was said to pursue women and squander money, Anthony castigated men whose profligacy created hardships for their dependent and powerless wives. Whereas Webster maintained that divorce laws had caused the fall of the Roman Empire, Anthony campaigned for the liberalization of divorce laws. Even in his oratorical style, Webster was Anthony's opposite. It is chiefly on his oratory that Stein draws for her characterization of him.

Daniel's first words in the play are not oratory but are the words of a child's nursery rhyme:

> He digged a pit, he digged it deep
>> he digged it for his brother.
> Into the pit he did fall in the pit
>> he digged for tother. (53)

This bit of doggerel, which Daniel repeats twice again in the scene, is interesting not only because it is about a "he" who stupidly digs his own grave (which Webster managed to do several times in his career) but also because it reveals that the monumental hero is at base nothing more than an overgrown child lisping nursery rhymes.

When next we hear from Daniel, he is seated beside Susan in Act 1, Scene 3. Daniel and Susan do not speak to each other, nor do they address the same audience. Susan speaks meditatively, half to herself, half to her companions, weighing the necessity for action against her desire for peace. "Shall I protest . . . I shall protest . . . shall I protest, shall I protest while I live and breathe" (59). Webster speaks as though from the Senate floor. He has matured since Scene 1, or at any rate, his language has. He is very conscious of his audience. He speaks with great formality:

> I can tell the honorable member once for all that he is greatly mistaken, and that he is dealing with one of whose temper and character he has yet much to learn.

Much indirection and pomposity:

> When this debate sir was to be resumed on Thursday it so happened that it would have been convenient for me to be elsewhere.

And some eloquence:

> The harvest of neutrality had been great, but we had gathered it all. (57–58)

Nine out of Daniel's fifteen speeches in this scene are taken intact from Daniel Webster's most famous senatorial speech, the 1830 debate with Senator Hayne of South Carolina over the Foote resolution "to consider limiting the sale of public lands."[26] The remaining speeches, save two, are also drawn from historical record. Webster's oratorical style was heightened by a liberal use of metaphor and dramatic emphasis. His words were chosen primarily for their effect. He was the master of ornate, Ciceronian rhetoric. His sentences were full and periodic; his diction was elevated and latinate. In other words, his rhetorical mode was patriarchal. Susan B. Anthony, on the other hand, was a plain speaker, as is Stein's Susan. In Act 1, Scene 3, standing opposite the posturing Daniel, she hesitates and changes direction as she speaks. Her words are not calculated but rather correspond moment by moment to her thoughts and feelings. Susan listens to an inner voice, unconscious of the effect on an audience of the words that record her thoughts. Hers is the speech of the mother; it is antipatriarchal.

Although Susan and Daniel do not at first address each other directly, Susan hears Daniel's every statement. For instance, when Daniel declares, "We have thus heard sir what a resolution is," Susan follows with "I am resolved." When Daniel says, "The honorable member complained that I had slept on his speech," Susan comments, "The right to sleep is given to no woman." Daniel, on the other hand, seems oblivious to Susan's presence. The only words of hers he appears to hear are her first: "I hear a sound." He counters: "I do not hear a sound. When I am told." His cryptic statement could mean either that he does not hear what is said to him, or that when he is told to turn a deaf ear, he does so. In either case, it is clear that, like the rich, Daniel Webster does not listen. He "sleeps" when others speak; he closes his ears to the sounds that others hear.

For Susan, the listener, Act 1, Scene 3 is an awakening. Daniel Webster's political power is (and was) derived from his ability to use the power of the spoken word, to avail himself of the rhetoric of patriarchy. Having made a decision to "fight for the right," to be a "martyr and live," not a "coward and die," Susan too must avail herself of the power of patriarchal language. She must set aside her private self and her private fears in order to become an effective public figure.

In the very next scene, Susan begins her lecture tours and, what Stein calls, her "education." She learns that, while it is always "agreeable" to be polite, it is not always productive:

> She often thought about politeness. She said politeness was so agreeable. Is it said Anne. Yes said Susan yes I think so that is to say politeness is agreeable that is to say it could be agreeable if everybody were polite but when it is only me, ah me, said Susan B. (59–60)

Politeness, a stereotypically female virtue, is no virtue at all in power politics. Susan also learns to speak more loudly, not only as loudly as she can, but even more loudly than she thinks she is able to speak. Soon Susan can declare, "they always listen to me" (61).

When next Susan joins Daniel Webster (Act 2, Scene 4), she is on the platform and he is down below. She speaks and he listens. She controls the order of events. Daniel addresses the audience only when Susan invites him to. Susan registers the change. "And now will Daniel Webster take the platform as never before" (70). To Susan's invitation Daniel responds with a double entendre which emphasizes, not his political power, but his sexual potency, suggesting that his political power has all along been a function of his masculinity, "Coming and coming alone, no man is alone when he comes, when he comes when he is coming he is not alone" (70). In her earlier encounter with Daniel, Susan had said, "I understand you undertake to overthrow my undertaking." Now she can declare, "I undertake to overthrow your undertaking."

Until now, I have emphasized Stein's use of historical sources in the creation of her characters, but as in *Doctor Faustus*, she revises the male-generated text (the historical record of public events and public speeches) and transforms it into a woman's story, both her own and Susan B. Anthony's. In the first place, of course, Daniel Webster (1782–1852) and Susan B. Anthony (1820–1906) were not exact contemporaries. Webster died twenty years before Anthony tested the Fifteenth Amendment in the courts. Stein also takes a similar liberty with history by having John Adams appear as a character. Moreover, Stein feels free to incorporate herself, her own acquaintances, and imaginary characters into the drama.

For Stein's play is only partly historical. This story, her story, is private and domestic as well as public and historical. Much of the play deals with the effects of history on the people who make it and who are made by it. This view of history gives us not only the public fact that Susan B. Anthony was unsuccessful in her opposition to the Fourteenth and Fifteenth Amendments, but also her private, bitterly ironic response to this fact.

In Act 2, Scene 7, Susan is joined by her companion Anne who congratulates her on the success of a recent speech. To Anne's praise, "Oh it was wonderful, wonderful, they listen to nobody the way they listen to you," Susan replies:

Yes it is wonderful as the result of my work for the first time the word male has been written into the constitution of the United States concerning suffrage. Yes it is wonderful. (79–80)

Susan's ironic interpretation of Anne's praise is echoed at the end of the scene by the chorus, as they evaluate Susan's success:

All the Chorus Men and Women.	Susan B. Anthony was very successful we are all very grateful to Susan B. Anthony because she was so successful, she worked for the votes for women and she worked for the vote for colored men and she was so successful, they wrote the word male into the constitution of the United States of America, dear Susan B. Anthony. Dear Susan B., whenever she wants to be and she always wants to be she is always so successful so very successful.
Susan B.	So successful. (83)

Stein represents not only the private sphere of Susan B. Anthony's story but also the private sphere in which most nineteenth-century women's lives were lived—the sphere of courtship and marriage. For like Marguerite in *Doctor Faustus*, the women in *The Mother of Us All* are involved in their own dramas of seduction. Susan B. Anthony and her companion, Anne, are the exceptions to this dramatic pattern because they have foregone sexuality (at least heterosexuality) and marriage for the demands of the cause. But for the rest of the characters, this play is as much about marriage as it is about suffrage. The play records a great deal of flirting, two full-fledged courtships, and one marriage. John Adams courts Constance Fletcher, and Jo the Loiterer courts and finally weds Indiana Elliot.

Before Jo meets his future bride, he tells his friend Chris the Citizen a story of a marriage he has imagined for himself:

Jo the Loiterer.	My wife, she had a garden.
Chris the Citizen.	Yes.
Jo the Loiterer.	And I bought one.
Chris the Citizen.	A wife.

No said Jo I was poor and I bought a garden. And then said Chris. She said, said Jo, she said my wife said one tree in my garden was her tree in her garden. And said Chris. Was it. Jo, We quarreled about it. And then said Chris. And then said Jo, we took a train and we went where we went. And then said Chris. She gave me a little package said Jo. And was it a tree said Chris. No it was money said Jo. And was she your wife said Chris, yes said Jo when she was funny, How funny said Chris. Very funny said Jo. Very funny said Jo. To be funny you have to take everything in the kitchen and put it on the floor, you have to take all your money and all your jewels and put them near the door you have to go to bed then and leave the door ajar. That is the way you do when you are funny. (54–55)

In Jo's story the wife begins the relationship in a position of economic superiority. She owns a garden; he does not. When Jo buys a garden he is his wife's economic equal. Then Jo and his wife have a quarrel over a tree, which is literally a disagreement over the right of possession, with the wife complaining that one of Jo's trees was taken from her garden. But the tree in the garden also suggests the consummation of the marriage, a suggestion continued in the metaphor of the train ride that the two take together. After the marriage is consummated, Jo's wife gives him a "little package" of "money," symbolizing her renunciation of economic independence. "And was she your wife," asks Chris. "Yes," replies Jo, "when she was funny." To be a wife, a woman must be "funny," which, as Jo describes it, means that she must relinquish all possessions—her money and her jewels—real and metaphorical (her virginity, the pearl of great price, being a jewel as well). The "funny" woman, having abandoned her worth on the floor near the door, must leave the door ajar and, dispossessed, vulnerable, and passive, must wait in bed for her husband.

Although one might deduce from Jo's previsualization of marriage that he would be a villainous suitor, Stein portrays him instead as a harmless, polite, rather compliant young man, much like Marguerite's man from over the seas. He is not one to force his will on anybody, male or female, and he is seemingly sympathetic to Susan's cause. His bride to be, Indiana Elliot, is a staunch feminist. It hardly seems that she will ever be "funny" enough to be Jo's wife. She claims to have had "no father"; she is not particularly eager to have a husband:

Jo the Loiterer.	I have just had an awful letter from home. . . .
Indiana Elliot.	What did they say.
Jo the Loiterer.	They said I must come home and not marry you.
Indiana.	Who ever said we were going to marry.
Jo the Loiterer.	Believe me I never did.
Indiana.	Disgrace to the cause of women, out.
	And she shoves him out. (71)

Though she finally agrees to marry, she continues to shove Jo about, even during the marriage ceremony:

Jo the Loiterer.   I tell her if she marries me do I marry her.

Indiana Elliot.   Listen to what he says so you can answer, have you the ring.

Jo the Loiterer.   You did not like the ring and mine is too large.

Indiana Elliot.   Hush.

Jo the Loiterer.   I wish my name was Adams.

Indiana Elliot.   Hush. (73)

Indiana is not to be bound by a ring, nor will she accept Jo's last name.

After the wedding, Jo confers with Susan at the window of her house over Indiana's refusal to take his name:

Indiana Elliot wants to come in, she will not take my name she says it is not all the same, she says that she is Indiana Elliot and that I am Jo, and that she will not take my name and that she will always tell me so. Oh yes she is right of course she is right it is not all the same Indiana Elliot is her name, she is only married to me, but there is no difference that I can see, but all the same there she is and she will not change her name, yes it is all the same. (77)

But even Indiana's strong will does not survive the literal marrying of personalities sanctioned by the marriage ceremony. Jo can announce in the next scene that Indiana "has decided to change her name." Indiana defends her decision:

Not because it is his name but it is such a pretty name, Indiana Loiterer is such a pretty name I think all the same he will have to change his name, he must be Jo Elliot, yes he must, it is what he has to do, he has to be Jo Elliot and I am going to be Indiana Loiterer, dear friends, all friends is it not a lovely name, Indiana Loiterer all the same. (82)

Jo the Loiterer seems willing to become Jo Elliot for Indiana's sake:

All right I never fight, nobody will know it's me, but what can I do, if I am not she and I am not me, what can I do, if a name is not true, what can I do but do as she tells me. (82)

Although Indiana has won several feminist battles, her marriage eventually causes her to lose the war. In the last scene of the play, she has "a great deal to say about marriage." Of all she says, her most telling comment is "how wonderful it is to be never married how wonderful" (85). By contrast, Jo (who has not taken her name as he promised) is quite delighted with marriage. He dances about with his old companion, Chris the Citizen, celebrating the realization of his dream of wedded bliss:

Jo the Loiterer.   Let us dance and sing, Chrissy Chris, wet and not in debt, I am a married man and I know how I show I am a married man. She votes, she changes her name and she votes. . . .

. . . .

Indiana Elliot.   I am a loiterer Indiana Loiterer and I can vote.
Jo the Loiterer.   You only have the name, you have not got the game. (87)

The outcome of the game to which Jo refers was already fixed when Indiana joined Constance Fletcher in an adoration of male greatness, "bowing low" to Daniel Webster in Act 2, Scene 4:

Dear man, he can make us glad that we have had so great so dear a man here with us now and now we bow before him here, this dear this dear great man. (70)

Susan admonished the two for making such a statement. "Hush, this is slush. Hush."

Susan has a different opinion of men than that of the women around her. She does not think men are "great." "Men can not count, they do not know that two and two make four if women do not tell them so" (73). According to Susan, men are inherently weak; their weakness turns to meanness when they are placed in positions of authority. She says, "There is a devil creeps into men when their hands are strengthened" (73). For all their conciliatory words and winning ways, for all their dependence on the women they love, men are not to be trusted once they are in power. If a woman does not stay clear of men, she will be placing herself in the hands of the devil, as Marguerite did when she fell into the arms of the seemingly kind and gentle man from over the seas.

Constance Fletcher, who seems on the surface more vulnerable than Indiana Elliot, survives the war between the sexes because she does not marry her suitor, John Adams. John begins his courtship of Constance with the unbending pride befitting his position as president of the United States and a male member of one of America's most illustrious families:

Dear Miss Constance Fletcher, it is a great pleasure that I kneel at your feet, but I am Adams, I kneel at the feet of none, not any one, dear Miss Constance Fletcher . . . if I had not been an Adams I would have kneeled at your feet. (62)

Throughout the play Adams's statements demonstrate his conviction of his own superiority: for example, "Do not pity me, I am an Adams and not pitiable" (63); or "I love women but I am never subdued by them never" (66); or "I never marry I have been twice divorced but I have never married . . . do you not admire me that I never can married be. I who have been twice divorced" (73). If one were to judge by language alone, one might agree that John Adams will never be subdued, never lose his individuality in a marriage. If one were to judge Constance Fletcher by her words alone, one might predict that she will easily be subdued by Adams. Her language is stereotypically feminine. She describes things as "pleasant," "lovely," "dear," and "beautiful." Her speech is often punctuated by the exclamations "dear me," "what a pity," and "bless you." She seems duly impressed by John Adams and the other dear and great men she encounters. But she is never impressed quite enough to marry one of them. And in her celibacy lies her strength. In the battle of the sexes, as Stein depicts it, sex is the ultimate weapon. The female maintains her supremacy only so long as she retains control of this weapon. In marriage she places the instrument of her own destruction in the hands of her enemy. By leading John Adams in an endless pursuit, Constance Fletcher avoids persecution. John Adams remains a fountain of unfulfilled desire as he declares, "Constance Fletcher dear Constance Fletcher noble Constance Fletcher and I spill I spill over like a thrill and a trill" (71). In the play's penultimate scene, John Adams is completely subdued. He enters, sees Constance Fletcher and says:

Dear friend beautiful friend, there is no beauty where you are not. . . . Dear friend I kneel to you because dear friend each time I see you I have never looked before, dear friend you are an open door. (81)

It is because Constance refused to place her jewels on the floor and open the door to him that John Adams kneels before her. Though he claims to perceive her now as an open door, he has yet to be given permission to enter the room.

Susan B. has also avoided marriage:

I am not married and the reason why is that I have had to do what I have had to do, I have had to be what I have had to be, I could never be one of two I could never be two in one as married couples do and can, I am but one all one, one and all one, and so I have never been married to any one. (75)

Stein's emphasis on the dangers of marriage for women is partly in keeping with Susan B. Anthony's own opinions on the matter. Anthony saw that marriage sapped a woman's energies because of the tremendous work load it imposed. Among her own associates, marriage inevitably diminished, if it did not end, active participation in "The Cause." She believed, moreover, that a woman was apt to lose her individuality in marriage. In a letter to Lydia Mott, Anthony wrote: "Such union [the spiritual or legal union of two human beings] . . . must bring an end to the free action of one or the other."[27] In an 1877 speech, "Homes of Single Women," Anthony maintained that inasmuch as custom and law defined marriage as the subjugation of the woman to the man, a "self-sustained" or a "self-respectful" woman must live without it despite the "superiority of the time-honored plan of making a home by the union of one man and one woman in marriage."[28] Anthony envisioned a necessary "epoch of single women," a transitional period during which women would achieve "equality at every point, morally, intellectually, physically, politically."[29] According to Anthony, only when full equality is achieved will marriage be a viable choice for a self-respecting woman.

Whereas Susan B. Anthony focused her critique of marriage on the ills of the social institution, ills created, sanctioned, and maintained by custom and law, Stein's critique of marriage, expressed through the character Susan B., focuses on the nature of the men whom women must marry. Therefore, Stein's Susan exhibits considerable hostility toward men. She describes them as "conservative . . . selfish . . . boresome . . . ugly, gullible, dull, monotonous, deceived, stupid, unchanging and bullies" (60–61). When she asks herself "what is man," she answers:

I do not say that they haven't kind hearts, if I fall down in a faint, they will rush to pick me up, if my house is on fire, they will rush in to put the fire out and help me, yes they have kind hearts but they are afraid. . . . They fear women, they fear each other, they fear their neighbor, they fear other countries and then they hearten themselves in their fear by crowding together and following each other, and when they crowd together and follow each other they are brutes, like animals who stampede, and so they have

written in the name male in the United States constitution, because
they are afraid of black men because they are afraid of women,
because they are afraid afraid. Men are afraid. (80)

In Susan's estimation, men are not only fearful but malevolent. When
Anne asks Susan why she does not publicly voice her criticisms of
men, Susan replies, "Why not, because if I did they would not listen
they not alone would not listen they would revenge themselves. Men
have kind hearts when they are not afraid but they are afraid afraid
afraid. I say they are afraid, but if I were to tell them so their kind-
ness would turn to hate" (80).

Susan B. Anthony's goals often were thwarted by men, but nowhere in the writings by and about Susan B. Anthony, not even in
her criticisms of particular men, can we find an attack against men
sui generis. Anthony never exhibited such virulence as does Stein's
heroine.[30]

Stein's Susan also exhibits what Richard Bridgman calls "disgust
at heterosexual coupling."[31] In this particular, too, Stein distorts the
historical record to convey her own reaction against the biological
destiny of her gender. Susan acknowledges the necessity of procreation for the continuance of the human race, especially the female
half. "If no one marries how can there be women to tell men, women
to tell men" (72). But Susan finds both mothering and copulation objectionable, albeit necessary. She objects to motherhood because it
dissipates the concentration on self that she deems a necessary condition for the individuation and protection of the female:

Susan B. Ah women often have not any sense of danger, after all
a hen screams pitifully when she sees an eagle but she is
only afraid for her children, men are afraid for themselves, that is the real difference between men and
women. (80)

As for copulation, Stein represents it throughout the play as a male's
intrusion through a door left ajar, or as his penetration of a veil, and
as a female's passive receptivity; as a male's appropriation of a female's jewel, and as a female's deprivation of power and possession.
Susan describes sex finally as a mystery and a horror. "It is a puzzle,
I am not puzzled but it is a puzzle, if there are no children there are
no men and women, and if there are men and women, it is rather
horrible, and if it is rather horrible, then there are children" (85).

If we examine Susan B. Anthony's statements about sex, we find
no such horror. In fact, her frankness, her refusal to be squeamish

about sexuality, led some of her contemporaries to describe her remarks on the subject as "gross" and "animal." In a letter to Elizabeth Cady Stanton, she wrote:

> To me it [sexual difference] is not coarse or gross, it is simply the answering of the highest and holiest function of the physical organism, that is that of *reproduction*. To be a *Mother*, or to be a *Father* is the last and highest wish of any human being, to *re-produce himself* or *herself*. The accomplish[ment] of this purpose is only through the meeting of the sexes. And when we come into the presence of one of the opposite sex, who embodies what to us seems the true and the noble and the beautiful, our souls are stirred, and whether we realize it or not, it is a thrill of joy that such qualities are reproducible *and* that we may be the *agents*, the *artists* in such re-production.[32]

Through the character of Susan, Stein announces her own conviction that the feminist struggle that ends in the marriage bed is an intolerable hypocrisy. In the prologue to *Fernhurst*, a novel which she wrote circa 1905, Stein evaluated Susan B. Anthony's cause as follows:

> The young woman of to-day up to the age of twenty one leads the same life as does her brother . . . conducting herself in all things as if there were no sex and mankind made all alike and traditional differences mere variations of dress and contour.
>
> I have seen college women years after graduation still embodying the type and accepting the standard of college girls—who were protected all their days from the struggles of the larger world and lived and died with the intellectual furniture obtained at their college—persisting to the end in their belief that their power was as a man's—and divested of superficial latin and cricket what was their standard but that of an ancient finishing school with courses in classics and liberty replacing the accomplishments of a lady. Much the same as a man's work if you like before he becomes a man but how much different from a man's work when manhood has once been attained.
>
> I wonder will the new woman ever relearn the fundamental facts of sex. Will she not see that college standards are of little worth in actual labor.
>
> I saw the other day a college woman resent being jostled by her male competitors in a rush for position—in spite of all training she was an American woman still, entitled to right and privileges and no more willing to adopt male standards in a struggle than her grandmother. She was neither less a woman or more dogged in battle though she had read latin and kicked a foot-ball.
>
> . . . .
>
> . . . What! does a reform start hopeful and glorious with a people to remake and all sex to destroy only to end in the same old homes with the same men and women in their very same place. Doctrines that have noble meanings often prove in action futile. . . . I have seen too much of successful reform to take off my hat and huzzah as it appears triumphant in eulogy and would do my little best with my complimenting neighbors that they should not applaud too loudly or fill their souls with too much hope. . . . Is it Susan

B. Anthony clamoring for the increase of the suffrage or John Marshall pleading for its restriction, I gaze at them and realise . . . that Miss Anthony and James Marshall are both eager that the truest justice should be granted to all.

Had I been bred in the last generation full of hope and unattainable desires I too would have declared that men and women are born equal but being of this generation with the college and professions open to me and able to learn that the other man is really stronger I say I will have none of it.[33]

This passage is a clear and direct statement of Stein's position on feminism—a position she occupied in 1905 and 1945, a position that is fictionalized in *Fernhurst* and dramatized in *The Mother of Us All*.

Because Susan B. Anthony believed that woman's inferior position was a result of social and political inequality, that is, institutional inequality, she believed in the efficacy of reform and in the importance of the political empowerment of women. So strongly did the suffragist believe that full equality would follow the enfranchisement of women and their participation in politics and governance, that she eventually concentrated her efforts on suffrage to the exclusion of other reforms. Like some of Anthony's contemporaries, most notably Elizabeth Cady Stanton, Gertrude Stein did not have Anthony's faith in the power of the vote. Nor did Stein have faith in the efficacy of the women's movement in a "man's world," a world in which men are different from women and women ill-equipped to deal with those differences. As *The Mother of Us All* shows, Gertrude Stein felt that suffrage was a dead end without a corresponding education in what Stein calls in *Fernhurst*, the "fundamental facts of sex," and without, as she says, a remaking of women, so that they would be willing to adopt male standards in their struggle.

In the last scene of *The Mother of Us All*, Susan appears as a statue in the Congressional Hall, one of a group representing the leaders of the suffrage movement. The spirit of the dead suffragist speaks through the statue. Although women now have the vote, Susan's tone is hardly celebratory. Her last words are a lament punctuated by long silences. Susan's obvious desolation has been interpreted, on the one hand, as representing the suffragist's regrets over the "martyrdom of her private self to the public good" which had resulted in "lessons unheard and unheeded,"[34] and on the other hand, as representing Stein's own doubts over the ultimate value of her martyrdom to aesthetic principles which had been largely misunderstood.[35]

However, Susan's closing lament is not Susan B. Anthony's assessment of her own life, nor is it exactly Stein's assessment of hers. Rather, it is Gertrude Stein's evaluation of Susan B. Anthony's life and ideals. In Stein's opinion, women could be free and equal only if they denied their heterosexuality and the gender identity that custom has determined is theirs, only if they concentrated on what Elizabeth Stanton had called in an 1892 speech to the House Judiciary Committee "The Solitude of Self." When Gertrude Stein abandoned her medical career in 1901, she also abandoned the women's movement. As Catharine Stimpson states, the prologue to *Fernhurst* marks Stein's separation of "herself from her sex in order to assail and herself enter a male world too strong for most women"—a world of the mind, not of the body, a world where, ideally, there are no sexual differences.[36]

In 1945, close to the end of her life, Stein again represented her separation from her sex. Susan's persistent doubts about the value of her cause are an expression of Stein's judgment of the women's movement, not a re-creation of Susan B. Anthony's misgivings. The suffragist had no such doubts. On her eighty-sixth birthday she affirmed, "Failure is impossible."[37] She believed from the beginning to the end that her cause was right; as she told a reporter, "I have never lost my faith, not for a moment in fifty years."[38] In contrast, Stein's Susan concludes that she has failed to change the nature of women's lives. She has regrets, but she acknowledges the impossibility of altering past actions. "We cannot retrace our steps, going forward may be the same as going backwards. We cannot retrace our steps, retrace our steps. All my long life, all my life, we do not retrace our steps" (87). In her long life Susan had endured "strife" because she had believed that her life of struggle could change the shape of the future and that the passage of laws could alter the fate of individuals. From her final vantage point, however, she looks out over the assembled characters and sees that their lives have not been changed by the enfranchisement of women. The vote has not stopped Lillian Russell from getting "old and fat"; it has not saved Constance Fletcher from becoming "blind as a bat"; it has not given Jenny Reefer hope; it has not provided Annie Hope with a belief nor stanched her tears. Indiana Loiterer and the others have not yet won the game.

The winning strategy is not marriage. Neither is it a singular devotion, like Susan B. Anthony's, to changing the rules of the game so that women can play. Rather, the winning strategy is, not surprisingly, Gertrude Stein's strategy—to play the game by existing rules and to beat the adversary on his own turf at his own game. This strategy is, in fact, closer to the young Marguerite's than it is to Susan B.'s. As Marguerite grasped the artificial viper, so Gertrude Stein grasped the pen. Like Marguerite, Stein ascended the throne of genius, a singular sun (the first one of her generation, she claimed, to create the modern composition in literature). Like Marguerite, Stein held court as people came by land and sea to visit her in her Paris apartment. Unlike Marguerite, Stein never quailed, never fell back into the arms of a protective male other, never dropped the pen.

By reincarnating Susan as a statue, Stein validates her own vocation, her choice of mind over body, of art over an active life as a feminist. The statue is not a real woman, as one bystander notes. But in marble and gold, Susan is "here," as no real woman could be. The statue stands aloof from the human beings whose destiny the living woman had tried to shape according to her ideals. As an inanimate incarnation of those ideals, the statue has more permanence than the suffragist, her ideals, or the people who lived and died by them—a truth which Susan had acknowledged long before her death:

> Susan B.   . . . Painters paint and writers write . . . and I I am
>   still alive.
> Anne.   They want you.
> Susan B.   And when they have me.
> Jenny Reefer.   Then they will want you again.
> Susan B.   Yes I know, they love me so, they tell me so, . . .
>   but I, I do not tell them so because I know, they
>   will not do what they could do and I I will be left
>   alone to die but they will not have done what I
>   need to have done to make it right that I live lived
>   my life and fight. (76)

Despite the statue's final lament, this play does not end in darkness. The spotlight shines. It calls our attention to the centrality and permanence of art. The last moment in *The Mother of Us All* belongs to the artists. The final image is the sculptor's. The final words are the playwright's. Through art, Susan B. Anthony will survive the final curtain, and Gertrude Stein with her. That is Stein's consolation, that is her triumph.

Epilogue: Contexts

When I first began to read and think about Stein's writing for the theater, I was struck by a statement from her lecture on plays: "Plays are either read or heard or seen" (94). Why, I wondered, does she separate these activities, giving them equal weight as alternative modes of experiencing a play? Or, does she give them equal weight? Does her arrangement of these alternatives privilege reading and, therefore, the text that is read? Is "seeing" last because to her mind it is the least of the three? Writing this book has been a process of discovering the answer to those questions, discovering the primacy of language and of the language-making activity of the poet in Stein's conception of theater art. As I pondered Stein's statements about theater, read her plays, and wrote about them, I was also led to discover, in the complex design which is the history of modern theater, an unexpected context for Stein's conception of theater.

When I began my work on Stein's plays, I had certain expectations about Stein's place in the history of the genre. These expectations arose from my knowledge of Stein's familiarity with the avant-garde theater of her time and from my knowledge of the staging her play texts had received in the avant-garde theater of my own time. I knew, for instance, that Stein had had frequent contact with Filippo Marinetti, Guillaume Apollinaire, André Breton, Jean Cocteau, and Tristan Tzara and had attended theater events they had scripted. I expected her plays to have some affinities with the plays these men wrote for the Cubo-Futurist, Surrealist, and Dadaist theaters, plays that created "a poetry of theatrical image" rather than "a poetry of words."[1] I knew that Stein had attended Serge Diaghilev's Ballets Russes, that she was a friend of Isadora Duncan and Raymond Craig, and that she knew set designers Eugène Berman and

Christian Berard (and, of course, Picasso, who designed the set for the ballet *Parade*). I therefore expected to see the impact on Stein's plays of these experimenters in the arts of "bodies in space" (dance and scenic design).

I knew also that Stein's *Doctor Faustus* was the first play staged by the Living Theater, and that Julian Beck had written of it, "It was like a manifesto and would always stand at the head of our work saying take the clue from this."[2] In fact, Stein's plays have most often been produced by theater groups like the Living Theater for whom the kinetic, visual, spatial "poetry" of theater is its most important attribute. I knew that among these groups and others, Stein's plays were, more often than not, accompanied by a musical score or by an almost balletic physical illustration. Furthermore, I knew that Stein's writing for the theater had been associated with Happenings by those most directly involved in them, like Dick Higgins, who writes: "She had a fragmented, grandiose concept of theater, a sort of instant theater, pageantlike but non-narrative, like the more imagistic and disciplined sort of happenings. These were her plays. Spoken arias to be orchestrated among sets of imagistic characters . . . an isolating of events to be treated musically and scored among available voices."[3] Since these contemporary avant-garde theater groups which adopted her texts and acknowledged her importance were the direct descendants, via Artaud, of the avant-garde theaters of the teens and twenties which Stein had attended, I assumed that this lineage was the appropriate historical context for Stein. However, despite Stein's familiarity with the originators of this avant-garde and despite her importance to their descendants, I did not find the affinities and connections I had expected to find.

In fact, Stein's approach to writing for the theater and her plays differ in two important respects from the avant-garde theater I have just been describing. Beginning with Alfred Jarry and continuing through the Dadaist, Futurist, Cubist, and Surrealist theaters, the central common preoccupation of these avant-gardes was to upset the audience, *épater la bourgeoisie*. Michael Kirby has identified this as the "antagonistic model" of the avant-garde theater.[4] Indeed, in Renato Poggioli's view, antagonism is a general characteristic of all avant-garde activity (the second of his four "moments" of the avant-garde). This avant-garde antagonism is directed against tradition and authority and against society itself. It leads to nihilism, "joy . . . in the act of beating down barriers, razing obstacles, destroying whatever stands in its way." The theater is an ideal forum for this kind of avant-garde activity because in the theater the antagonistic artist can personally confront the "collective individual called the public" whom he seeks to upset and whose values he seeks to destroy.[5] While Stein's plays, like those of the antagonistic avant-garde, present us with an unfamiliar and potentially alienating theater experience, I would argue that they are not antagonistic or nihilistic. Whereas the Surrealists sought to terrorize, the Dadaists to offend, and the Futurists to shock the audience, Stein wished for a theater experience that would allow the audience to "rest untroubled" in the performance of the play. Her discussion in her lecture "Plays" of the troubling "nervousness" caused by "the fact that your emotional time as an audience is not the same as the emotional time of the play" indicates that Stein saw herself as writing plays that might heal the breach (symbolized by the curtain) between what is going on on the stage and what the audience is experiencing (94–95). We can say of Stein, as she does of Picasso, that she is a "creator," an artist in the avant-garde because she is, like Picasso, "the first of [her] contemporaries to be conscious of what is happening to [her] generation."[6] The work that results from this consciousness may be "disconcerting," may even appear "ugly." The public may initially reject the creator's "composition" as meaningless, but Stein believes that if the creator perseveres in expressing her vision, she will find her audience. The public will catch up to the creator and will accept what it once rejected, recognizing it as a realization and representation of things as they are and even seeing the beauty in that representation. Stein's faith in this "reunion" of artist and audience sets her apart from her contemporaries in the antagonistic avant-garde theater.

The second and more important difference between Stein and the antagonistic avant-garde playwrights resides in the texts themselves and in the importance accorded to the text by the playwright. For the antagonistic avant-garde, the text is of minimal importance. Instead, the visual, spatial, and dynamic elements of performance are valorized. In fact, these theater texts are almost always antiliterary (either implicitly or explicitly). It is a short and not surprising step from these theaters to that envisioned by Antonin Artaud, a theater without texts, without language.

Language being of paramount importance in the theater Stein envisioned, she would have more readily endorsed Maurice Maeterlinck's view of theater than Cocteau's. Maeterlinck wrote: "I myself take little or no interest in the practical side of dramatic life. I always enjoy reading a play far more than I do seeing it acted, for on the stage the delicate symbolic essence of what every thoughtful writer wishes to convey cannot escape."[7] Cocteau, on the other hand, wrote: "The fact is that I am trying to substitute a 'theater poetry' for the usual 'poetry in the theater.' 'Poetry in the theater' is a delicate lace, invisible at any considerable distance. 'Theater poetry' should be a coarse lace, a lace of rigging, a ship upon the sea. *Wedding Party* can be as terrifying as a drop of poetry under the microscope. The scenes fit together like the words of a poem."[8] To point to an affinity between Maeterlinck and Stein is not to make a case for Symbolist influence on her; nevertheless, placing Stein in the Symbolist context allows us to see that Stein's plays do not reduce language to just another element in a pure theater event, like color, shape, music, and movement. Rather, Stein's plays bring poetry into the theater.

Although Stein's is a theater of language, it has very little in common with the theater of language created by Samuel Beckett. Stein is sometimes, and mistakenly, placed in the camp of Beckett and Eugène Ionesco. However, this, too, is a misleading contextualization of Stein's plays. Whereas Beckett focuses on the language and language-making activities of society, Stein focuses on the language and language-making activity of the poet—the interior and isolated activity of poiesis. Whereas Beckett's is a "discourse of versimilitude"—to use Julia Kristeva's phrase[9]—Stein's is a discourse of defamiliarization. Beckett uses language to represent an existential condition; he creates characters who are distinguishable from one another by their speech and who exist in a stage reality also created by language. For Stein, on the other hand, language represents nothing other than itself. Words are the things that are exhibited during the performance of a Stein play. The text-making activity of the poet and her language play become a theatrical event; grammar becomes a theatrical device. Although both Beckett and Stein create theaters of language, Beckett's is created out of "his ever-renewed sense of the failure of language," as Andrew Kennedy points out,[10] whereas Stein's is created out of a belief in the sacredness and perfection of language as it is used by the poet and in its ability to successfully communicate the poet's composition to an audience. Kristeva concludes that Beckett's theater is "edged with debility."[11] One can only stand outside language and criticize it for so long before one is reduced to silence (which was exactly the direction in which Beckett's theater headed). Stein's plays, on the other hand, are full of possibility for the future of language in the theater.

The possibilities which Stein's work suggests have been explored and realized by a number of American avant-garde language artists: David Antin, John Cage, Allan Kaprow, Dick Higgins, Jackson MacLow, Jerome Rothenberg, and Richard Foreman, to name the most obvious. Of these, only Foreman could rightly be called a playwright. The rest are variously called process poets, performance artists, exemplativists, language poets, oral poets, and text-sound poets.

Like Stein, they have an interest in the interplay between textuality and performance; their work, like Stein's, is metatextually self-conscious, routinely collapsing the boundaries between literary criticism and practice. All believe in the theatricality, the performability of language and in the performative and transformative power of "poetry."

That they are all Americans is no surprise; so was Stein. The latter is not so obvious a statement as it might at first seem. Stein is often seen as part of European literary modernism and avant-gardism, and her American roots are sometimes ignored or dismissed as insignificant. Without wishing to downplay European influences on Stein, I believe that it was her nationality and her grounding in the American literary tradition that separated her quite profoundly from her European contemporaries (with the exception of Picasso, an exception Stein explains with a theory about the natural affinity between Spaniards and Americans based on certain geographical similarities between their two countries).[12]

In his brilliant book, *Poet's Prose: The Crisis in American Verse*, Stephen Fredman traces an American tradition of poet's prose which embraces not only Stein and some of the avant-garde performance poets she influenced, but also Ralph Waldo Emerson, Walt Whitman, William Carlos Williams, Robert Creeley, and John Ashbery. Fredman calls Stein the "notable presence" and "shadow heroine" of his book.[13] Like Fredman, I believe that Stein had more in common with Emerson, Whitman, and Williams than with Cocteau, Breton, Tzara, and Marinetti. Briefly, Fredman argues that the American tradition of poet's prose is composed of two strains—the meditative and the oratorical—both of which were rooted in Puritanism, flourished in the nineteenth century (especially in Emerson's poetic prose), and bore fruit in the twentieth-century poet's prose of Williams, Ashbery, Creeley, and David Antin (the "heroes" of Fredman's book).[14] The meditative strain manifests itself in the "self-dramatizing, self-questioning" characteristics of twentieth-century poet's prose, and the oratorical strain manifests itself in the value that these poets place on speech and its generative effect. Regarding the oratorical strain, Fredman writes, "[The] orator provides a model of the poet who speaks from the inherently risky moment of lived time, bringing to it a heightened attention to the act of composition."[15] The poets Fredman discusses, all of whom were directly influenced by Stein, as he points out, chose to "investigate how things arise from the matrix of language ... the ultimate goal [of their prose] would be an interchange with language so highly charged that one would apprehend the absolutely constitutive role language plays in the world."[16] Like their European counterparts, Charles Baudelaire and Arthur Rimbaud, these American poets deconstruct or abandon genre, turning instead to the fundamental poetic medium, language, which then "becomes the object of investigation or creation."[17] Unlike their European counterparts, however, they attempt to reconcile private language play and exploration with communal expression. These poets ask their prose, which Fredman correctly describes as "drastic . . . at war with decorum and intensely private,"[18] to "articulate a shared world."[19] While it is beyond the scope of this book to discuss Stein as an American writer, I would like to suggest that what set her apart from her European contemporaries was a characteristically American belief that a text which records a personal, private, poetic investigation of language can also reflect the truths of the poet's generation and can successfully communicate those truths to the public.

Since this is a book about Stein's plays, I would like to focus here on the ways in which her writing for the theater prefigures the work of poets who consistently write on the borders between textuality and performance. Richard Foreman has written that Stein's contribution to theater was to replace "narrative with process concerns" as a way of dealing with the problem of traditional theater ("pre-Steinian theatre" as Foreman calls it). The problem of this "pre-Steinian" theater was that it "always asked the spectator to THINK the implications of the presented moment in terms of the past and future moment." Stein's theater had the "technique required to make the richness and density be IN the moment."[20] Stein achieves this "presentness" in her plays by recording poiesis, the play of the poet with language. In Stein's theater we can experience this play of language because the language that plays before us is a record and reenactment of the language play of the poet. Although Stein's plays become printed texts and rehearsed reenactments, they continue to seem like improvisations because they were originally improvised and because Stein strives to preserve the improvisational process in the printed and enacted product.

Stein's metadramatic confrontation with the rules, problems, limits, and paradoxes of dramatic art are also part of the process her plays record and enact. Her plays embody her critique of, her ideas about, and her deconstruction of the genre she was working in. Stein's plays are at once works of art and works of dramatic criticism. She is at once creating and thinking about creation. In this respect, Stein's plays anticipate a kind of writing that Dick Higgins has called "exemplative art." In exemplative art, "the idea is developed through its embodiment in the actual work."[21] Higgins explains:

We do not love a Gertrude Stein play or a Shakespeare sonnet or a recent John Cage orchestra piece because it is perfect—but because we feel our lives in these works. . . . They do not symbolize life, but they actively reflect it— suggest and propose things about it. . . . [In exemplative art] all form is a process of notation. . . . The audience sees or senses the bare bones of the work along with the flesh . . . and the act of . . . assembling is part of the work. . . . In exemplative art, then, the artist will always be involved in the ongoing process of inventing new forms.[22]

Higgins points to the fact that all such work, even the most static, involves some aspect of performance.

During her improvisational private poiesis, Stein is always conscious of the inevitable rehearsal and public performance awaiting her play. She is as committed to this performance as she is to poiesis, though the clash of the two creates a tension in her plays, sometimes resolved, sometimes not. Furthermore, Stein is as committed to the text—language as product (the words on a page, the grammar of the sentence)—as she is to either of the performances—the improvised writing process or the rehearsed speaking by performers. This three-fold commitment, too, creates a tension that she is not always able to resolve. However, it is her willingness to engage in these conflicts, these simultaneous commitments, which makes her a sort of "heroine" to poets/performers who are currently engaged in similar activities. I am thinking particularly of David Antin, whose talk poetry dwells in the same twilight zones between text, poiesis, and performance. Antin improvises as he talks his poems during a performance. Later he transcribes and publishes them as texts, all the while trying to preserve the oral, improvisational, and performative quality of the original discourse. Stein improvises as she writes her plays, later relinquishing them to performance, all the while trying to preserve the improvisational and performative quality of the original discourse. For both Stein and Antin (and for other oral and performance poets), textuality and performance are inextricably bound in one complex creative act.

Julia Kristeva has argued that "modern theater does not take (A) place," that it "no longer exists outside the text."[23] In Stein's plays, however, the modern theater does exist. Stein's work with drama dissolved the boundaries between theater and poetry, allowing a kind of hybrid of the two to come into being, a performed poetry, at once textual and theatrical. Thus, her plays show a way through the crisis of language in the theater, which Kristeva argues is a failure of demonstration, not of representation, "because nothing represents better than language."[24] Stein, too, believed in the representative capability of language both in the theater and out. In the theater, Stein used language to represent the moment of utterance and the process of playing; in the theater that moment and that process can take (a) place, can be demonstrated by the performers and observed by the audience. Stein's writing for the theater made a new theater language and a new place for language in the theater. This is her contribution to the history of the genre.

Appendix: A Chronology of Gertrude Stein's Published Plays

Because Gertrude Stein's plays depart so radically from conventional drama, it is not always immediately obvious which of her texts are plays. Works included on this chronological list of Stein's published plays meet some combination of the following criteria: (1) the title or subtitle indicates that the text is an opera or play, or the text appears in the volume *Operas and Plays*; (2) the text consists entirely of conversational address and response; (3) the text is divided into a main text and a side text which includes character ascriptions, act/scene divisions, and scene setting; or (4) the text is metadramatic and contains internal evidence that it was written for eventual performance.

The plays are listed according to the year of their composition based on the chronology established by Richard Bridgman in Appendix C of *Gertrude Stein in Pieces*. In identifying the volumes in which these plays appear, I have used the following abbreviations:

BTV	*Bee Time Vine*
G&P	*Geography and Plays*
GSFR	*Gertrude Stein First Reader*
LO&P	*Last Operas and Plays*
O&P	*Operas and Plays*
PL	*Painted Lace*
P&P	*Portraits and Prayers*
ROAB	*Reflection on the Atomic Bomb*
SIM	*Stanzas in Meditation*
SW	*Selected Writings*
UK	*Useful Knowledge*

The abbreviated name of the volume is followed by the page number on which the play begins.

1913

    What Happened. A Five Act Play, G&P, 205.
    White Wines, G&P, 210.
    Old and Old, O&P, 219.
    A Curtain Raiser, G&P, 202.

1915

    Not Sightly. A Play, G&P, 290.
    Farragut or A Husband's Recompense, UK, 5.
    This One Is Serious, PL, 20.
    He Didn't Light the Light, PL, 17.
    Independent Embroidery, PL, 81.
    He Said It. Monologue, G&P, 267.

1916

    For the Country Entirely. A Play in Letters, G&P, 227.
    Henry and I, PL, 273.
    Water Pipe, ROAB, 31.
    Ladies' Voices. Curtain Raiser, G&P, 203.
    Every Afternoon. A Dialogue, G&P, 254.
    Advertisements, G&P, 341.
    Do Let Us Go Away. A Play, G&P, 215.
    Let Us Be Easily Careful, PL, 35.
    Bonne Annee. A Play, G&P, 302.
    Captain Walter Arnold. A Play, G&P, 260.
    In Memory (Polybe Silent), PL, 29.
    Please Do Not Suffer. A Play, G&P, 262.
    I Like It to Be a Play. A Play, G&P, 286.
    A Very Good House, PL, 26.
    Turkey and Bones and Eating and We Liked It. A Play, G&P, 239.
    I Often Think about Another, PL, 32.
    A Collection, G&P, 23.
    I Must Try to Write the History of Belmonte, G&P, 70.
    Look at Us, PL, 259.
    Mexico. A Play, G&P, 304.
    Decorations, BTV, 185.
    A Poem about Waldberg, G&P, 166.

1917

    The King or Something (The Public Is Invited to Dance), G&P, 122.
    Counting Her Dresses. A Play, G&P, 275.

Have They Attacked Mary. He Giggled (A Political Caricature), SW, 533.
An Exercise in Analysis. A Play, LO&P, 119.
I Can Feel the Beauty, PL, 84.
Will We See Them Again, PL, 275.
Why Can Kipling Speak, BTV, 188.

1918

In Their Play, BTV, 206.
What Is the Name of a Ring, BTV, 180.
Can You See the Name, BTV, 204.
Making Sense, BTV, 202.
Work Again, G&P, 392.

1919

Accents in Alsace. A Reasonable Tragedy, G&P, 409.
A Poetical Plea, BTV, 195.
The Work, BTV, 189.
Tourty or Tourtebattre. A Story of the Great War, G&P, 401.

1920

A Movie, O&P, 395.
Photograph. A Play, LO&P, 152.
Scenery, BTV, 217.
Coal and Wood, PL, 3.
A Circular Play. A Play in Circles, LO&P, 139.
Woodrow Wilson, UK, 104.

1921

B. B. or The Birthplace of Bonnes, P&P, 162.
Capture Splinters, BTV, 218.
Reread Another. A Play to Be Played Indoors or Out. I Wish to Be a School, O&P, 123.

1922

Objects Lie on a Table. A Play, O&P, 105.
Saints and Singing. A Play, O&P, 71.
Lend a Hand or Four Religions, UK, 170.

1923

A List, O&P, 89.
Capital Capitals, O&P, 61.
Jonas Julian Caesar and Samuel, PL, 286.

A Village. Are You Ready Yet Not Yet. A Play in Four Acts. Paris: Galerie Simon, 1928.

Am I to Go or I'll Say So, O&P, 113.

1927

Four Saints in Three Acts. An Opera to Be Sung, O&P, 11.

1928

A Lyrical Opera Made by Two. To Be Sung, O&P, 49.

Paiseu. A Play. A Work of Pure Imagination in Which No Reminiscences Intrude, LO&P, 155.

A Bouquet. Their Wills, O&P, 195.

1929

Film. Deux soeurs qui ne sont pas soeurs, O&P, 399.

1930

Parlor. A Play between Parlor of the Sisters and Parlor of the Earls, O&P, 325.

At Present. A Play. Nothing but Contemporaries Allowed, O&P, 315.

Madame Recamier. An Opera, O&P, 355.

They Weighed Weighed-Layed. A Drama of Aphorisms, O&P, 231.

To Help. In Case of Accident, SIM, 253.

An Historic Drama in Memory of Winnie Elliot, LO&P, 182.

Will He Come Back Better. Second Historic Drama. In the Country, LO&P, 189.

Third Historic Drama, LO&P, 195.

Politeness, PL, 142.

Louis XI and Madame Giraud, O&P, 345.

Play I [–III], LO&P, 200.

1931

Say It with Flowers, O&P, 331.

The Five Georges, O&P, 293.

Lynn and the College of France, O&P, 249.

They Must. Be Wedded. To Their Wife. A Play, O&P, 161.

Civilization. A Play in Three Acts, O&P, 131.

1932

A Play without Roses. Portrait of Eugene Jolas, P&P, 200.

A Play of Pounds, LO&P, 239.

A Manoir. An Historical Play in Which They Are Approached More Often, LO&P, 277.

Short Sentences, LO&P, 317.

A Play. A Lion. For Max Jacob, P&P, 28.

1933

Byron a Play. But Which They Say Byron a Play, LO&P, 333.

1936

Listen to Me. A Play, LO&P, 387.

A Play Called Not and Now, LO&P, 422.

1937

Daniel Webster. Eighteen in America. A Play, ROAB, 95.

1938

Doctor Faustus Lights the Lights, LO&P, 89.

Lucretia Borgia. A Play, ROAB, 118.

1941

Lesson Sixteen. A Play, GSFR, 42.

1943

In a Garden. A Tragedy in One Act, GSFR, 59.

Three Sisters Who Are Not Sisters. A Melodrama, GSFR, 63.

Look and Long. A Play in Three Acts, GSFR, 73.

1944–1946

Yes Is for a Very Young Man, LO&P, 1.

The Mother of Us All, LO&P, 52.

Notes

Introduction

1. In *Gertrude Stein in Pieces*, Richard Bridgman discusses the conversation plays in his chapter 6 and devotes part of his chapter 9 to *Four Saints in Three Acts*. He treats *Listen to Me* and *Not and Now* in chapter 13, *Doctor Faustus Lights the Lights* in chapter 14, and *Yes Is for a Very Young Man* and *The Mother of Us All* in chapter 15 (New York: Oxford University Press, 1970). Marianne DeKoven considers the conversation plays in her chapter "Voices and Plays" and looks at *Four Saints in Three Acts* in the chapter "Landscape," largely devoted to a discussion of *Lucy Church Amiably* (*A Different Language: Gertrude Stein's Experimental Writing* [Madison: University of Wisconsin Press, 1983]). Randa Dubnick briefly considers several plays in "The List in Stein's Plays, Poems, and Portraits," in her *The Structure of Obscurity: Gertrude Stein, Language, and Cubism* (Urbana: University of Illinois Press, 1984). Michael Hoffman provides an introduction to both "dialogue" and "landscape" plays in his book *Gertrude Stein* (Boston: Twayne, 1976). Allegra Stewart offers a Jungian reading of *Doctor Faustus Lights the Lights* (*Gertrude Stein and the Present* [Cambridge, MA: Harvard University Press, 1967]). Donald Sutherland devotes a chapter of *Gertrude Stein: A Biography of Her Work* to a survey of the plays (New Haven, CT: Yale University Press, 1951), and Norman Weinstein focuses on *Four Saints in Three Acts* in a chapter of *Gertrude Stein and the Literature of Modern Consciousness* (New York: Frederick Ungar, 1970).

2. Bruce Kellner, ed., *A Gertrude Stein Companion: Content with the Example* (Westport, CT: Greenwood Press, 1988), 8.

3. DeKoven, *A Different Language*, xv.

4. John Hyde Preston, "A Conversation," *The Atlantic Monthly*, August 1935, 187.

5. Betsy Alayne Ryan, *Gertrude Stein's Theatre of the Absolute* (Ann Arbor, MI: UMI Research Press, 1984), 40.

6. Ibid.

7. Gertrude Stein, "Plays" in *Lectures in America* (1935; reprint, Boston: Beacon Press, 1985), 118, hereafter cited as "Plays."

8. DeKoven, *A Different Language*, xx.

9. Ibid., xiv.

10. Harriet Scott Chessman, *The Public Is Invited to Dance: Representation, the Body, and Dialogue in Gertrude Stein* (Stanford, CA: Stanford University Press, 1989), 112.

11. Ibid., 3.

12. Ibid., 6.

13. Ibid., 8.

14. DeKoven, *A Different Language*, xvi.

15. Chessman, *The Public Is Invited to Dance*, 6–7.

16. Lionel Abel, *Metatheatre: A New View of Dramatic Form* (New York: Hill and Wang, 1963), 60.

17. Richard Hornby, *Drama, Metadrama, and Perception* (Lewisburg, PA: Bucknell University Press, 1986), 31.

18. Patrice Pavis, *Languages of the Stage: Essays in the Semiology of the Theatre* (New York: Performing Arts Journal Publications, 1982), 79.

19. James L. Calderwood, *Shakespearan Metadrama* (Minneapolis: University of Minnesota Press, 1971), 5.

20. Susan Wittig, "Toward a Semiotic Theory of the Drama," *Educational Theatre Journal*, 26 (December 1974): 453–454.

21. Calderwood, *Shakespearean Metadrama*, 7.

22. Pavis, *Languages of the Stage*, 75.

23. David Antin, "Some Questions about Modernism," *Occident*, 8 (Spring 1974): 31.

24. Pierre Larthomas, *Le Langage dramatique: sa nature, ses procédés* (Paris: Presses Universitaires de France, 1980), 25.

25. Keir Elam, "Language in the Theater," *Sub-Stance*, 18/19 (1977): 158.

26. Jindřich Honzl, "The Hierarchy of Dramatic Devices," in *The Semiotics of Art: The Prague School Contributions*, ed. Ladislav Matejka and Irwin R. Titunik (Cambridge, MA: MIT Press, 1976), 127.

27. Pavis, *Languages of the Stage*, 80.

28. Jiří Veltruský, "Dramatic Text as a Component of Theater," in *Semiotics of Art*, 115.

29. Honzl, "The Hierarchy of Dramatic Devices," 127.

30. Veltrusky, "Dramatic Text," 115.

31. André Helbo, "Theater as Representation," *Sub-Stance*, 18/19 (1977): 176.

32. Elam, "Language in the Theater," 146–147.

33. Pavis, *Languages of the Stage*, 80.

34. Calderwood, *Shakespearean Metadrama*, 55.

Chapter 1

1. Stein, "Plays," 118.

2. All three plays were published in *Geography and Plays* (1922; reprint, New York: Something Else Press, 1968).

3. Jindřich Honzl points to this primacy of action in theater art. He likens action to an electric "current," flowing through and unifying "word, actor, costume, scenery, and music" ("Dynamics of the Sign in the Theater," in *Semiotics of Art*, 91).

4. Stein, *Geography and Plays*, 205–209.

5. Ibid., 210–214.

6. Wendy Steiner, *Exact Resemblance to Exact Resemblance: The Literary Portraiture of Gertrude Stein* (New Haven, CT: Yale University Press, 1978), 105.

7. Stein, "Plays," 119.

8. Gertrude Stein, "Jenny, Helen, Hannah, Paul and Peter" (1912), MS. 43, Notebook 1, Gertrude Stein Papers, Yale Collection of American Literature, Beinecke Library (hereafter, YCAL).

9. Stein, MS. 43, Notebook 2, YCAL.

10. Stein, MS. 43, Notebook 2, YCAL.

11. Stein, MS. 43, Notebook 3, YCAL.

12. Stein, MS. 43, Notebook 5, YCAL.

13. Harriet Chessman suggests that Stein created an entire "poetics of dialogue." The Steinian dialogue, Chessman writes, "occurs in myriad forms, yet it is arguably ceaseless, as the primary structure out of which her writing is generated" (61). This view is not incompatible with my own interpretation of Stein's metadramatic writing. In the conversation plays, the dialogue is literally a verbal exchange between or among separate voices. On one level, this exchange is, as Chessman argues, an "enactment of a *relationship between* two figures" (65). On another level, as I show in this chapter, Stein's dialogic exchanges—her conversations—play with and are played off against the conventions of dramatic dialogue. This implicit self-reflexive "play" becomes increasingly explicit in Stein's writing for the theater (a phenomenon I discuss in detail in subsequent chapters). One could characterize this metadramatic activity in Stein's plays as her "dialogue" with the genre and as one of the "myriad forms" of dialogue which Chessman suggests we can find in Stein's work.

14. Bridgman, *Stein in Pieces*, 149.

15. I am using these terms in the sense suggested by Barbara Herrnstein Smith in *On the Margins of Discourse* (Chicago: University of Chicago Press, 1978). According to Smith, a natural utterance is "a historical *event* . . . it occupies a specific and unique point in time and space [and] thus cannot recur, for it is historically unique." A printed text which is a record of vocal utterance is not a natural utterance, but the transcription of one. Poems and plays are fictive utterances, representations of natural utterance. A written text can only be a natural utterance at the moment of its composition (15–28).

16. Stein, "Plays," 119.

17. Ibid., 118–119.

18. Ibid., 122.

19. Gertrude Stein, *Bee Time Vine and Other Pieces* (New Haven, CT: Yale University Press, 1953), 204–205.

20. Occasionally, in other conversation plays we find some side text. For example, *Counting Her Dresses* (*Geography and Plays*, 275–285) is divided into forty-two parts, each part composed of from one to seven acts. But these textual divisions do not suggest the commencement or completion of an "action." Rather, each part indicates that the subject of the dialogue has changed; within the parts each act is a new line of dialogue. Thus, the only "acts" in the play are speech acts. In other plays with act or scene divisions (*For the Country Entirely* [*Geography and Plays*, 227–238] and *Turkey and Bones and Eating and We Liked It* [*Geography and Plays*, 239–253]), the numbering and distribution of parts is random and disordered. Thus, acts do not mark the orderly unfolding of an action through its constituent parts, nor do

scenes suggest the temporal or spatial location of acts. On rare occasions, Stein will slip something that could be construed as a stage direction into a conversation play. So, for instance, in *Every Afternoon* we find these two lines: "A great many people come in. / A great many people come in" (*Geography and Plays*, 257). Here we recognize the conventional language of stage directions, the verb in the simple present. However, these lines are not set off from the rest of the text, and thus, they seem to be, not stage directions, but declarations in an ongoing conversation. In this period Stein also wrote a few plays with tentative character ascriptions, the names enclosed in parentheses as though they were incidental and expendable. I deal with these "characters" in greater detail later in this chapter.

21. Stein, *Geography and Plays*, 304.

22. Gertrude Stein, *Painted Lace and Other Pieces* (New Haven, CT: Yale University Press, 1955), 17.

23. Stein wrote most of the conversation plays while she and Alice Toklas lived in Mallorca where they had sought refuge from the war. As she wrote in a 1915 letter to Henry McBride, she was "inspired by the Mallorcans a very foolish lot of decayed pirates with an awful language" (18 September 1915, YCAL). Undoubtedly, Stein's reproduction in her conversation plays of the give-and-take of social conversation was inspired in part by the conversations taking place around her and by the necessary concentration on domestic life occasioned by her temporary exile from Paris. References to Mallorca, Mallorcans, islands, water, and war and its privations dot the conversation plays. While such biographical information can only enrich our reading of the plays, it should not distract us from the fact that these plays are more concerned with the form of conversation than with its meaning and that, for Stein at this time, a word's possible reference to an extralinguistic situation was its least important feature.

24. Gertrude Stein, *Mexico*, in *Geography and Plays*, 304–330. Further page references appear in the text.

25. This focus on the spelling of words in the text is an isolated example of an activity that would become characteristic of Stein's landscape plays: the inclusion of the act of writing the play in the action of the play (see chapter 2, pp. 27–34 and 50–62, and chapter 3, pp. 81–96).

26. Keir Elam, *The Semiotics of Theatre and Drama* (London: Methuen, 1980), 151.

27. Keir Elam points out that metalanguage and the existence of words as words make language "a phenomenon of interest or concern in its own right: language itself . . . may be presented as the object of discourse" (*The Semiotics of Theatre and Drama*, 154).

28. Gertrude Stein, *Every Afternoon*, in *Geography and Plays*, 254.

29. Gertrude Stein, *He Said It*, in *Geography and Plays*, 271.

30. Gertrude Stein, *Counting Her Dresses*, in *Geography and Plays*, 280.

31. Gertrude Stein, *Captain Walter Arnold*, in *Geography and Plays*, 260.

32. Stein, *Every Afternoon*, 256.

33. Although Stein leaves out the extralinguistic situation, it necessarily affects the dialogue and is, therefore, implied by the dialogue. In commenting on and in staging these plays, one will naturally be tempted to uncover the action within the extralinguistic situation, the action that the dialogue implies, for as much as Stein tries to reduce action to mere "potentiality,"

action is the one irreducible element of theatrical art. As Veltruský notes, "Without acting there is no theater, at least no drama-performing theater" (114).

34. Stein, *Every Afternoon*, 258.

35. John L. Styan, *Drama, Stage, and Audience* (London: Cambridge University Press, 1975), vii.

36. Elam, *The Semiotics of Theatre and Drama*, 138.

37. Ibid., 182.

38. Bridgman, *Stein in Pieces*, 58.

39. An actor need not be a human being. Honzl writes that the actor could be "a piece of wood," a mechanical puppet or simply a voice, but whatever it is, it must represent "someone," must signify "a role in a play" ("Dynamics of the Sign in the Theater," 75).

40. Gertrude Stein, *Please Do Not Suffer*, in *Geography and Plays*, 265–266. Further page references appear in the text.

41. Susanne Langer, *Feeling and Form: A Theory of Art* (New York: Charles Scribner's Sons, 1953), 310.

42. Gertrude Stein, *Do Let Us Go Away. A Play*, in *Geography and Plays*, 215–216.

43. In this instance it does indeed seem as though Stein is addressing her "characters," with the unassigned portions of dialogue being Stein's and the rest belonging to the named characters.

44. According to Betsy Alayne Ryan's "Chronological List of Productions" (*Gertrude Stein's Theatre of the Absolute*, 165–189), only one of the conversation plays, *For the Country Entirely*, has been produced in its entirety without operatic adaptation.

45. When she began writing plays in 1913, Stein sent several of them to Mabel Dodge in the hopes that she would be able to get them produced in New York. Dodge suggested, in a letter, that the plays be published instead. Stein was intransigent: "No decidedly not. I do *not* want the plays published. They are to be kept to be *played*" (Gertrude Stein to Mabel Dodge, [?] 1913, YCAL). In 1914, when Donald Evans of Claire Marie Press wrote to her asking to publish a volume of her plays, he had been forewarned of her probable refusal. He wrote, "I should very much like to publish in volume form the plays of yours that Mrs. Dodge has told me about. Will you let me do it? . . . Mr. Van Vechten told me he thought you might not wish the plays published before you had them produced here. My bringing out the volume, my dear Miss Stein, would not in any way hurt the producing value; in fact, it would stimulate interest in their production in the theatre" (18 February 1914, *The Flowers of Friendship: Letters Written to Gertrude Stein*, ed. Donald Gallup [New York: Alfred A. Knopf, 1953], 95–96). Stein was not reassured and sent instead the manuscript of *Tender Buttons*. She may have felt, because of promises made by Henry McBride, the art critic of the *New York Sun*, that production was imminent and so worth waiting for. On 28 August 1913, McBride had written to Stein as follows regarding the plays she had shown him earlier: "I wanted to read those plays over again and talk with you about them. That man Willis Polk of San Francisco is already returned to Paris. He is Chief of the Architectural Commission for the Fair, and has some influence in a general way I imagine. I told him that the Fair should stage your plays, and that Society that plays out in the Forest should know of you. To do the

gentleman justice, I must say, his eyes sparkled at the idea. . . . In the meantime, I still think they should be done next winter in New York, and if they are done, I hope I shall be allowed to help. If you see anything in the Fair, let me know and I'll nab Polk. He gave me the idea that the San Franciscans would love to be up to date or a little ahead of it, if possible" (Gallup, *Flowers of Friendship*, 83). Nothing ever came of all these promises, and the plays in question were eventually published in 1922 in *Geography and Plays* without having been produced. Stein's desire to have her plays staged never abated, although its gratification was almost always as elusive as it had been in 1913 and 1914. Stein objected not only to the idea of her plays as closet dramas, available only in print, but also to the idea that they were esoteric pieces suitable only for minimal staging in the context of a literary salon or art society. In 1944 and 1945 Stein made various efforts to have *Yes Is for a Very Young Man* produced, even translating it into French for a proposed production at the American Army University at Biarritz, under her supervision. However, she abruptly withdrew her play from this production because, as Alice Toklas explained in a letter to Carl Van Vechten, she objected to a "workshop performance," that is, a production without scenery and to a "hand-picked audience" (19 November 1946, *Staying on Alone: Letters of Alice B. Toklas*, ed. Edward Burns [New York: Vintage Books, 1975], 32). These incidents suggest that Stein wrote her plays for production not for publication.

46. Elam, *The Semiotics of Theatre and Drama*, 142.

Chapter 2

1. Yi-Fu Tuan, "Thought and Landscape: The Eye and the Mind's Eye," in *The Interpretation of Ordinary Landscapes*, ed. D. W. Meinig (New York: Oxford University Press, 1979), 90.

2. John Brinckerhoff Jackson, *The Necessity for Ruins and Other Topics* (Amherst: University of Massachusetts Press, 1980), 69.

3. John A. Jakle, *The Visual Elements of Landscape* (Amherst: University of Massachusetts Press, 1987), 8.

4. Edward Relph, *Rational Landscapes and Humanistic Geography* (London: Croom Helm, 1981), 22.

5. John Brinckerhoff Jackson, *Discovering the Vernacular Landscape* (New Haven, CT: Yale University Press, 1984), 156.

6. For a discussion of landscape painting as "the transient captured," see Kenneth Clark, *Landscape into Art* (New York: Harper and Row, 1976). John Brinckerhoff Jackson discusses landscape as a place "where we speed up or retard or divert the cosmic program and impose our own," in *Discovering the Vernacular Landscape*, 156.

7. Lawrence Kornfeld, "From a Director's Notebook: How the Curtain Did Come: Conflict and Change: The Theatre of Gertrude Stein," *Performing Arts Journal*, Spring 1976: 33–35.

8. Gertrude Stein, *A List*, in *Operas and Plays* (1932; reprint, Barrytown, NY: Station Hill Press, 1987), 89. Further page references appear in the text.

9. In manuscript Stein writes "Susan Mabel Martha and Susan, Mable and Martha and a father," changing the spelling of the second "Mabel," an "error" Toklas corrected when she typed the manuscript. The "misspelling"

shows that orthography also plays a part in our recognition of people by their names (Stein, *A List*, MS. 286, YCAL).

10. In 1923, the year that Stein wrote *A List*, Pitoeff staged Pirandello's *Six Characters in Search of an Author* for Parisian audiences. In Stein's play, as in Pirandello's, the existence, identity, and fate of the characters depend on the playwriting activities of the author, and this connection between authorial process and dramatic realization is debated by characters in both plays. There is no evidence that Stein saw Pirandello's play, but if she did not see it, she would have inevitably heard about it since it was a much discussed *succès de scandale*. The metatextual affinities between *A List* and *Six Characters in Search of an Author* are undeniable. The interesting difference between the two plays is that the fate of Pirandello's characters depends on the form in which the playwright will cast their story, whereas the fate of Stein's characters is determined by language itself, by the way words appear in the playwright's text.

11. In her article "*Stanzas in Meditation*: The Other Autobiography," Ulla Dydo explains that these wordplays with the names "May, Mary, May Mary, and Mabel" and the words "marry" and "may" were probably coded references to Stein's early love affair (1901–1903) with a Bryn Mawr graduate, May Bookstaver (Mabel having been a rival for Bookstaver's affection). Alice Toklas knew nothing of the affair in 1923, so in typing up the manuscript of *A List*, she was unknowingly transcribing her lover's references to a former lover. Dydo writes that when Toklas did learn of the affair in 1932, "she became, as she put it, 'paranoid about the name May,' " and that her paranoia caused Stein to try to eliminate all forms of the word "may" from *Stanzas in Meditation*, the text she was working on at the time (*Chicago Review*, 35 [Winter 1985]: 11–14).

12. Keir Elam points out that foregrounded language is always "conspicuous"—noticeable and almost palpable ("Language in the Theater," 148).

13. Roman Ingarden, *The Literary Work of Art: An Investigation on the Borderlines of Ontology, Logic, and Theory of Literature*, trans. George C. Grabowicz (Evanston, IL: Northwestern University Press, 1973), 61.

14. Calderwood, *Shakespearean Metadrama*, 72.

15. Gertrude Stein, "Portraits and Repetition," in *Lectures in America*, 196–198.

16. Elam, "Language in the Theater," 153.

17. Bridgman, *Stein in Pieces*, 172.

18. Steiner, *Exact Resemblance to Exact Resemblance*, 165.

19. Gertrude Stein, *A Circular Play. A Play in Circles*, in *Last Operas and Plays* (1949; reprint, New York: Vintage Books, 1975), 139–151.

20. Gertrude Stein, *Saints and Singing*, in *Operas and Plays*, 86.

21. Gertrude Stein, *A Village. Are You Ready Yet Not Yet. A Play in Four Acts* (Paris: Galerie Simon, 1928).

22. Gertrude Stein, *Four Saints in Three Acts*, MS. 349, Notebook 1, YCAL.

23. Stein, *Four Saints in Three Acts*, in *Operas and Plays*, 11. Further page references appear in the text.

24. Stein, *Four Saints in Three Acts*, MS. 349, Notebook 1, YCAL.

25. Virgil Thomson, *Virgil Thomson* (New York: Alfred A. Knopf, 1966), 175.

26. Gertrude Stein, *The Autobiography of Alice B. Toklas* (1933; reprint, New York: Vintage Books, 1961), 79.

27. Gertrude Stein to Mabel Dodge, [?] February 1913, YCAL.

28. Joseph Kerman, *Opera As Drama*, rev. ed. (Berkeley and Los Angeles: University of California Press, 1988), 159.

29. Patrick J. Smith, *The Tenth Muse: A Historical Study of the Opera Libretto* (New York: Alfred A. Knopf, 1970), 282–283.

30. Gertrude Stein, *Mme Recamier An Opera*, MS. 416, YCAL.

31. Gertrude Stein to Henry McBride, 25 October 1930, YCAL.

32. Stein, *Lectures in America*, 125.

33. Gertrude Stein, *Everybody's Autobiography* (1937; reprint, New York: Vintage Books, 1973), 114.

34. Ibid., 48, 98, 111, and 193.

35. Ibid., 194; and *Lectures in America*, 125, 129, and 131.

36. Stein, *Everybody's Autobiography*, 283.

37. Thomson, *Virgil Thomson*, 158.

38. Ibid., 90–91.

39. Gertrude Stein to Virgil Thomson, 30 March 1927, YCAL.

40. Gertrude Stein to Virgil Thomson, 23 May 1927, YCAL.

41. Gertrude Stein to Virgil Thomson, 7 June 1927, YCAL.

42. Thomson, *Virgil Thomson*, 46.

43. Ibid., 89.

44. Ibid., 96.

45. Gertrude Stein to Virgil Thomson, 3 January 1927, YCAL.

46. Stein, *The Autobiography of Alice B. Toklas*, 228.

47. Stein, *Everybody's Autobiography*, 317.

48. Virgil Thomson, *The Musical Scene* (New York: Alfred A. Knopf, 1945), 297–298.

49. Thomson, *Virgil Thomson*, 105.

50. Ibid., 90.

51. Kathleen Hoover and John Cage, *Virgil Thomson: His Life and Music* (New York: Thomas Yoseloff, 1959), 144.

52. Gertrude Stein, *Capital Capitals*, in *Operas and Plays*, 61.

53. Hoover and Cage, *Virgil Thomson*, 145.

54. Thomson, *Virgil Thomson*, 105.

55. Kenneth Burke, "Two Brands of Piety," review of *Four Saints in Three Acts, The Nation*, 28 February 1934: 256–257.

56. Stark Young, "One Moment Alit," review of *Four Saints in Three Acts, The New Republic*, 7 March 1934: 105.

57. Edith J. R. Isaacs, review of *Four Saints in Three Acts, Theatre Arts Monthly*, April 1934: 246.

58. Gilbert Seldes, "Delight in the Theatre," review of *Four Saints in Three Acts, Modern Music*, March–April 1934: 138.

59. Brooks Atkinson, review of *Four Saints in Three Acts, New York Times*, 17 April 1952.

60. Miles Kastendieck, "A Unique Experience: A Handsome Show," review of *Four Saints in Three Acts, New York Journal American*, 17 April 1952.

61. Calderwood, *Shakespearean Metadrama*, 72.

62. Colin Cherry, *On Human Communication: A Review, a Survey, and a Criticism* (Cambridge, MA: MIT Press, 1966), 80.

63. Michael Kirby, *A Formalist Theatre* (Philadelphia: University of Pennsylvania Press, 1987), 26.

64. Ibid., 22.

65. Elizabeth Burns, *Theatricality: A Study of Convention in the Theatre and in Social Life* (London: Longman, 1972), 146.

66. Bridgman, *Stein in Pieces*, 187.

67. Stein, "Plays," 130.

68. Ibid., 130.

69. Gertrude Stein, typescript of a tape-recorded interview with William Lundell for the National Broadcasting Company, New York, 12 October 1934, YCAL. Stein's memory is confused here. She finished the manuscript at the end of July, which is not exactly the end of summer although the grass in this urban park could certainly have been yellow in July.

70. In addition to being Stein's lament about the yellowing grass and the end of summer, "alas" is also a pun on Alice. Ulla Dydo, Harriet Chessman, and Neil Schmitz have all discussed the omnipresence of Alice Toklas in Stein's writing. As Schmitz writes, "She is addressed, cited, quoted . . . [she is] everywhere *in* Gertrude Stein's text, variously figured, differently inscribed" (*Of Huck and Alice: Humorous Writing in American Literature* [Minneapolis: University of Minnesota Press, 1983], 202). By singing in *Four Saints* to Alice/alas (the witness to the writing and the companion of the writer), Stein further draws creation and performance together.

71. Stein, "Plays," 129.

72. Gertrude Stein, *How to Write* (1931; reprint, West Glover, VT: Something Else Press, 1973), 39. Further page references appear in the text.

73. Stein, *Lectures in America*, 93.

74. Roman Jakobson, *Verbal Art, Verbal Sign, Verbal Time*, ed. Krystyna Pomorska and Stephen Rudy (Minneapolis: University of Minnesota Press, 1985), 20.

75. In *Everybody's Autobiography*, writing about the Thomson/Grosser production of *Four Saints* and about the Gerald Berners staging of *A Wedding Bouquet*, Stein comments, "As yet they have not yet done any of mine without music to help them. They could though and it would be interesting but no one has yet" (194).

76. Jakobson, *Verbal Art*, 20.

77. Gertrude Stein, *Paiseu. A Work of Pure Imagination in Which No Reminiscences Intrude*, in *Last Operas and Plays*, 155–181. Further page references appear in the text.

78. *Paiseu* has suggestions both of *paix*, "peace," and *pays*, "country." *Pays* is the root of words derived from the French *paix*, as in "paisiblement." In Old French, according to Larousse *Ancien Français*, the words based on the root are closer in spelling to Stein's word "Paiseu," e.g., *pais* (noun) from the Vernacular Latin *pagensem*, "habitant of a *pagus* or canton"; *paisier* (verb) or *paisivement* (adverb) from the Latin *pax* or *pacem*.

79. Gertrude Stein, *They Must. Be Wedded. To Their Wife*, in *Last Operas and Plays*, 229. Further page references appear in the text.

80. Gertrude Stein, *An Historic Drama in Memory of Winnie Elliot*, in *Last Operas and Plays*, 182–184.

81. Gertrude Stein, *The Five Georges*, in *Operas and Plays*, 293.

82. Gertrude Stein, *They Weighed Weighed-Layed*, in *Operas and Plays*, 231–248.

83. Gertrude Stein, *A Manoir*, in *Last Operas and Plays*, 281. Further page references appear in the text.

Chapter 3

1. Stein, "Plays," 102. Further page references appear in the text.
2. As it happens, the heyday of theatrical illusionism in America coincided with Stein's adolescence. In New York in 1869, Edwin Booth installed hydraulic machinery in his newly built theater. In 1880 Steel Mackaye built Madison Square Garden and, in 1883, the Lyceum Theatre, both of which used indirect lighting and an elevator stage. These technical innovations permitted greater realism in staging. David Belasco, who had used real sheep in an 1879 staging of *The Passion Play* in San Francisco, was at the peak of his touring company career at the turn of the century. Though Stein does not mention having attended *The Passion Play* or any of Belasco's other productions, she went so regularly to the theater throughout her childhood and adolescence that she would almost certainly have seen his and other similarly illusionistic performances.
3. Honzl, "Dynamics of the Sign in the Theater," 90.
4. Stein, *Everybody's Autobiography*, 194.
5. Gertrude Stein, *The Geographical History of America or the Relation of Human Nature to the Human Mind* (1935; reprint, New York: Vintage Books, 1973), 76–77. Further page references appear in the text.
6. Johan Huizinga, *Homo Ludens: A Study of the Play-Element in Culture*, trans. R. F. C. Hull (London: Routledge and Kegan Paul, 1949), 4.
7. Ibid., 119.
8. Gertrude Stein, *Byron a Play*, in *Last Operas and Plays*, 335.
9. Donald Baker, "A Structural Theory of Theatre," *Yale/Theatre*, 8 (Fall 1976): 56–57.
10. "Wilder" could also refer to Thornton Wilder whom Stein had met on her American tour and who subsequently became a good friend. Changing "wild" to "wilder," then, would not only introduce a comparison but also a proper name—the name of an identifiable person, a social acquaintance, a speaker, a person with a "human nature."
11. Gertrude Stein, *A Play Called Not and Now*, in *Last Operas and Plays*, 422. Further page references appear in the text.
12. Gertrude Stein, *Composition as Explanation* (London: Hogarth Press, 1926); reprinted in *Look at Me Now and Here I Am: Writings and Lectures 1909–45*, ed. Patricia Meyerowitz (Harmondsworth: Penguin Books, 1971), 29.
13. Gertrude Stein, *Listen to Me*, in *Last Operas and Plays*, 387. Further page references appear in the text.
14. Stein, *Everybody's Autobiography*, 242–243.
15. Ibid., 193.

Chapter 4

1. The play called *Lucretia Borgia* (written in 1938) and the plays that appear in *The Gertrude Stein First Reader and Three Plays* (written between 1941 and 1943) are not part of this trend toward conventional, autobiographical

writing. *Lucretia Borgia* is a very short play which Robert Haas suggests was a "preparation piece for the later novel *Ida*" (*Reflection on the Atomic Bomb: Volume I of the Previously Uncollected Writings of Gertrude Stein*, ed. Robert Bartlett Haas [Los Angeles: Black Sparrow Press, 1973], 94). The plays in the *First Reader* are concerned with the connection between plays and children's play. They are subtitled "a tragedy," "a melodrama," and "a play," but the texts resemble traditional nursery rhymes, songs, and games for children—hence the title of the book (*The Gertrude Stein First Reader and Three Plays* [Boston: Houghton Mifflin, 1948]).

2. Gertrude Stein to Carl Van Vechten, 29 January 1931, *The Letters of Gertrude Stein and Carl Van Vechten 1913–1946*, ed. Edward Burns (New York: Columbia University Press, 1986), 1:235.

3. Gertrude Stein to William Aspenwall Bradley, 25 May 1934, YCAL.

4. DeKoven, *A Different Language*, xviii.

5. Ibid., xx.

6. Gallup, *Flowers of Friendship*, 329.

7. Gerald Berners to Gertrude Stein, 28 April 1938, YCAL.

8. Gerald Berners to Gertrude Stein, 3 December 1939, Gallup, *Flowers of Friendship*, 346.

9. Gertrude Stein to Carl Van Vechten, 20 June 1938, Burns, *The Letters of Gertrude Stein and Carl Van Vechten*, 2:598.

10. For a complete history of Doctor Faustus, see Frank Baron, *Doctor Faustus from History to Legend* (Munich: Wilhelm Fink Verlag, 1978).

11. Gertrude Stein, *Doctor Faustus Lights the Lights*, in *Last Operas and Plays*, 89. Further page references appear in the text.

12. In her Jungian analysis of *Doctor Faustus Lights the Lights*, Allegra Stewart argues that Stein uses this composite name to identify Marguerite as "a compound symbol of the eternal feminine in all its aspects." Stewart breaks the "compound symbol" into these parts: "Marguerite, feeling; Ida, sensation; Helena, thought; Annabel, intuition" (162–163). My discussion of *Doctor Faustus* shows that Stein's characterization of Marguerite is, in fact, antithetical to the eternal feminine ideal of submission and passive suffering (represented in Goethe's *Faust* by Margarete/Gretchen) and to the "fallen" version of that ideal, the woman who destroys men through her beauty and desirability (represented in Goethe's *Faust* by Helen). Both aspects of the eternal feminine imply that women are powerless except insofar as they can manipulate men (for good or ill) through their good influence or through their sexual attractiveness. Stein's heroine is Faustus's equal, and her power is like a man's. Even though she eventually succumbs to the pressures of the feminine ideal, she does not, herself, represent that ideal. (For a full discussion of the eternal feminine as a "German variant of a common topos in Western literature," see Susan L. Cocalis and Kay Goodman, "The Eternal Feminine Is Leading Us On," introduction to *Beyond the Eternal Feminine: Critical Essays on Women and German Literature*, ed. Susan L. Cocalis and Kay Goodman [Stuttgart: Akademischer Verlag, 1982].)

13. Nancy A. Kaiser, "Faust/Faustine in the Nineteenth Century: Man's Myth, Women's Places," in *Our Faust? Roots and Ramifications of a Modern German Myth*, ed. Reinhold Grimm and Jost Hermand (Madison: University of Wisconsin Press, 1987), 65.

14. Margaret B. Guenther, "*Faust*: The Tragedy Reexamined," in *Beyond the Eternal Feminine*, ed. Susan L. Cocalis and Kay Goodman, 97.

15. Guenther, *"Faust,"* 76.

16. A. N. Okerlund, " 'Be Silent Then, for Danger Is in Words': The Intellectual Folly of Dr. Faustus," in *Reinterpretations of Marlowe's Faustus: A Collection of Critical Essays,* ed. Ghanshiam Sharma (Delhi: Doaba House, 1984), 189.

17. Ibid., 206.

18. Gertrude Stein, *The Mother of Us All,* in *Last Operas and Plays,* 53. Further page references appear in the text.

19. Stein had thoroughly researched Anthony's life and historical period, drawing on books at the American Library in Paris and even sending to the New York Public Library for materials. She wrote to Thomson on 24 September 1945, "They seem to be sending me from the New York public library all the literature of the period, if it comes off it will be a most erudite opera" (YCAL).

20. Quoted in Katharine Anthony, *Susan B. Anthony: Her Personal History and Her Era* (Garden City, NY: Doubleday, 1954), 90.

21. Quoted in Kathleen Barry, *Susan B. Anthony: A Biography of a Singular Feminist* (New York: New York University Press, 1988), 310–311.

22. Irving H. Bartlett, *Daniel Webster* (New York: W. W. Norton and Co., 1978), 295.

23. Ibid., 10.

24. Ibid., 3.

25. Ibid., 7.

26. Ibid., 114.

27. Quoted in Barry, *Susan B. Anthony,* 119.

28. Susan B. Anthony and Elizabeth Cady Stanton, *Correspondence, Writings, Speeches,* ed. Ellen Carol DuBois (New York: Schocken Books, 1981), 147–148.

29. Ibid., 148.

30. Although Anthony worked with and was helped by a number of men she regarded as friends, her experience with the Fourteenth Amendment and with the betrayal of the women's movement by the very men whom she had assisted and whose reciprocal assistance she had relied on left her wary of trusting men to further her cause. See William O'Neill, *Everyone Was Brave: A History of Feminism in America* (New York: Quadrangle, 1969), 17. See also Ellen Carol DuBois, *Feminism and Suffrage: The Emergence of an Independent Women's Movement in America, 1848–1869* (Ithaca, NY: Cornell University Press, 1978), chapters 2 and 3. Anthony did not dislike men as a group or as friends, but she did come to mistrust them as political allies.

31. Bridgman, *Stein in Pieces,* 341.

32. Susan B. Anthony to Elizabeth Cady Stanton, 29 September 1857, *Correspondence, Writings, Speeches,* 67.

33. Gertrude Stein, *Fernhurst, Q.E.D., and Other Early Writings* (New York: Liveright, 1971), 3–8.

34. Louis R. Barbato, "Gertrude Stein's Operas," paper presented at the seminar "Ellen Glasgow and Gertrude Stein: A Centennial Retrospective," annual meeting of the Modern Language Association of America, New York, 27 December 1974.

35. Carl Van Vechten, Introduction, *Last Operas and Plays,* by Gertrude Stein, xii.

36. Catharine R. Stimpson, "The Mind, the Body, and Gertrude Stein," *Critical Inquiry* 3 (Spring 1977): 497.

37. Ida Husted Harper, *The Life and Work of Susan B. Anthony* (Indianapolis, IN: The Hollenbeck Press, 1908), 3:1409.

38. Ibid., 3:1308.

Epilogue

1. Tom F. Driver, *Romantic Quest and Modern Query: A History of the Modern Theatre* (New York: Delacorte Press, 1970), 140.

2. Julian Beck, "Storming the Barricades," Introduction, *The Brig*, by Kenneth H. Brown (New York: Hill and Wang, 1965), 8.

3. Dick Higgins, *Horizons: The Poetics and Theory of the Intermedia* (Carbondale: Southern Illinois University Press, 1984), 2.

4. Kirby, *A Formalist Theatre*, 97.

5. Renato Poggioli, *The Theory of the Avant-Garde*, trans. Gerald Fitzgerald (Cambridge, MA: Harvard University Press, 1968), 25–26.

6. Gertrude Stein, *Picasso: The Complete Writings*, ed. Edward Burns (Boston: Beacon Press, 1985), 63.

7. Quoted in John Stokes, *Resistible Theatres* (London: Paul Elek Books, 1972), 171.

8. Jean Cocteau, "Preface to *The Eiffel Tower Wedding Party*," in *The Infernal Machine* (New York: New Directions, 1963), 156.

9. Julia Kristeva, "Modern Theater Does Not Take (A) Place," *SubStance*, 18/19 (1977): 131.

10. Andrew Kennedy, *Six Dramatists in Search of a Language* (London: Cambridge University Press, 1975), 135.

11. Kristeva, "Modern Theater," 131.

12. In *Picasso* Stein writes, "While other Europeans were still in the nineteenth century, Spain because of its lack of organization and America by its excess of organization were the natural founders of the twentieth century" (39). According to Stein, Spaniards and Americans are further united by their rejection of the reality perceived by the rest of the world: "Spaniards and Americans are not like Europeans, they are not like Orientals, they have something in common, that is they do not need religion or mysticism not to believe in reality as all the world knows it, not even when they see it. In fact reality for them is not real and that is why there are skyscrapers and American literature and Spanish painting and literature" (44). Later she explains that in Spain, "the landscape and the houses do not agree, the round is opposed to the cube, the movement of the earth is against the movement of the houses. . . . Spaniards know that there is no agreement, neither the landscape with the houses, neither the round with the cube . . . it was natural that a Spaniard should express this in the painting of the twentieth century, the century where nothing is in agreement. . . . America and Spain have this thing in common, that is why Spain discovered America and America Spain, in fact it is for this reason that both of them have found their moment in the twentieth century" (54–57).

13. Stephen Fredman, *Poet's Prose: The Crisis in American Verse* (London: Cambridge University Press, 1983), 151 n. 15; 140.

14. Fredman's discussion of "these two central strands in American discourse . . . oratory and meditation" (34) draws on David Porter's treatment of the sources of Emerson's poetic prose in *Emerson and Literary Change* (Cambridge, MA: Harvard University Press, 1978).

15. Ibid., 35.

16. Ibid., viii.

17. Ibid., 4–5.

18. Ibid., 4.

19. Ibid., 8.

20. Richard Foreman, *Plays and Manifestos*, ed. Kate Davy (New York: New York University Press, 1976), 145–146.

21. Dick Higgins, "An Exemplativist Manifesto," in *The Word and Beyond: Four Literary Cosmologists* (New York: The Smith, 1982), 103.

22. Ibid., 105.

23. Kristeva, "Modern Theater," 131.

24. Ibid.

Works Cited

Abel, Lionel. *Metatheatre: A New View of Dramatic Form*. New York: Hill and Wang, 1963.

Anthony, Katharine. *Susan B. Anthony: Her Personal History and Her Era*. Garden City, NY: Doubleday, 1954.

Anthony, Susan B., and Elizabeth Cady Stanton. *Correspondence, Writings, Speeches*, edited by Ellen Carl DuBois. New York: Schocken Books, 1981.

Antin, David. "Some Questions about Modernism." *Occident*, 8 (Spring 1974): 7–38.

Atkinson, Brooks. Review of *Four Saints in Three Acts*, by Gertrude Stein. *New York Times*, 17 April 1952.

Baker, Donald. "A Structural Theory of Theatre." *Yale/Theatre*, 8 (Fall 1976): 55–61.

Barbato, Louis R. "Gertrude Stein's Operas." Paper presented at the seminar "Ellen Glasgow and Gertrude Stein: A Centennial Retrospective." Annual meeting of the Modern Language Association of America, New York, 27 December 1974.

Baron, Frank. *Doctor Faustus from History to Legend*. Munich: Wilhelm Fink Verlag, 1978.

Barry, Kathleen. *Susan B. Anthony: A Biography of a Singular Feminist*. New York: New York University Press, 1988.

Bartlett, Irving H. *Daniel Webster*. New York: W. W. Norton and Co., 1978.

Beck, Julian. "Storming the Barricades." Introduction to *The Brig*, by Kenneth H. Brown. New York: Hill and Wang, 1965.

Bridgman, Richard. *Gertrude Stein in Pieces*. New York: Oxford University Press, 1970.

Burke, Kenneth. "Two Brands of Piety." Review of *Four Saints in Three Acts*, by Gertrude Stein. *The Nation*, 28 February 1934: 256–258.

Burns, Edward, ed. *The Letters of Gertrude Stein and Carl Van Vechten 1913–1946*, 2 vols. New York: Columbia University Press, 1986.

———. *Staying on Alone: Letters of Alice B. Toklas*. New York: Vintage Books, 1975.

Burns, Elizabeth. *Theatricality: A Study of Convention in the Theatre and in Social Life*. London: Longman, 1972.

Calderwood, James L. *Shakespearean Metadrama*. Minneapolis: University of Minnesota Press, 1971.

Cherry, Colin. *On Human Communication: A Review, a Survey, and a Criticism.* Cambridge, MA: MIT Press, 1966.

Chessman, Harriet Scott. *The Public Is Invited to Dance: Representation, the Body, and Dialogue in Gertrude Stein*. Stanford, CA: Stanford University Press, 1989.

Clark, Kenneth. *Landscape into Art*. New York: Harper and Row, 1976.

Cocalis, Susan L., and Kay Goodman. "The Eternal Feminine Is Leading Us On." Introduction to *Beyond the Eternal Feminine: Critical Essays on Women and German Literature*, edited by Susan L. Cocalis and Kay Goodman. Stuttgart: Akademischer Verlag, 1982.

Cocteau, Jean. "Preface to *The Eiffel Tower Wedding Party*." In *The Infernal Machine*. New York: New Directions, 1963.

DeKoven, Marianne. *A Different Language: Gertrude Stein's Experimental Writing*. Madison: University of Wisconsin Press, 1983.

Driver, Tom F. *Romantic Quest and Modern Query: A History of the Modern Theatre*. New York: Delacorte Press, 1970.

Dubnick, Randa. *The Structure of Obscurity: Gertrude Stein, Language, and Cubism*. Urbana: University of Illinois Press, 1984.

DuBois, Ellen Carol. *Feminism and Suffrage: The Emergence of an Independent Women's Movement in America, 1848–1869*. Ithaca, NY: Cornell University Press, 1978.

Dydo, Ulla. "*Stanzas in Meditation*: The Other Autobiography." *Chicago Review*, 35 (Winter 1985): 4–20.

Elam, Keir. "Language in the Theater." *Sub-Stance*, 18/19 (1977): 139–161.

———. *The Semiotics of Theatre and Drama*. London: Methuen, 1980.

Foreman, Richard. *Plays and Manifestos*, edited by Kate Davy. New York: New York University Press, 1976.

Fredman, Stephen. *Poet's Prose: The Crisis in American Verse*. London: Cambridge University Press, 1983.

Gallup, Donald, ed. *The Flowers of Friendship: Letters Written to Gertrude Stein*. New York: Alfred A. Knopf, 1953.

Guenther, Margaret B. "*Faust*: The Tragedy Reexamined." In *Beyond the Eternal Feminine: Critical Essays on Women and German Literature*, edited by Susan L. Cocalis and Kay Goodman. Stuttgart: Akademischer Verlag, 1982.

Harper, Ida Husted. *The Life and Work of Susan B. Anthony*, vol. 3. Indianapolis, IN: The Hollenbeck Press, 1908.

Helbo, André. "Theater as Representation." *Sub-Stance*, 18/19 (1977): 172–181.

Higgins, Dick. "An Exemplativist Manifesto." In *The Word and Beyond: Four Literary Cosmologists*. New York: The Smith, 1982.

———. *Horizons: The Poetics and Theory of the Intermedia*. Carbondale: Southern Illinois University Press, 1984.

Hoffman, Michael J. *Gertrude Stein*. Boston: Twayne, 1976.

Honzl, Jindřich. "Dynamics of the Sign in the Theater." In *The Semiotics of Art: The Prague School Contributions*, edited by Ladislav Matejka and Irwin R. Titunik. Cambridge, MA: MIT Press, 1976.

———. "The Hierarchy of Dramatic Devices." In *The Semiotics of Art: The Prague School Contributions*, edited by Ladislav Matejka and Irwin R. Titunik. Cambridge, MA: MIT Press, 1976.

Hoover, Kathleen, and John Cage. *Virgil Thomson: His Life and Music*. New York: Thomas Yoseloff, 1959.

Hornby, Richard. *Drama, Metadrama, and Perception*. Lewisburg, PA: Bucknell University Press, 1986.

Huizinga, Johan. *Homo Ludens: A Study of the Play-Element in Culture*, translated by R. F. C. Hull. London: Routledge and Kegan Paul, 1949.

Ingarden, Roman. *The Literary Work of Art: An Investigation on the Borderlines of Ontology, Logic and Theory of Literature*, translated by George C. Grabowicz. Evanston, IL: Northwestern University Press, 1973.

Isaacs, Edith J. R. Review of *Four Saints in Three Acts*, by Gertrude Stein. *Theatre Arts Monthly*, April 1934: 246.

Jackson, John Brinckerhoff. *Discovering the Vernacular Landscape*. New Haven, CT: Yale University Press, 1984.

———. *The Necessity for Ruins and Other Topics*. Amherst: University of Massachusetts Press, 1980.

Jakle, John A. *The Visual Elements of Landscape*. Amherst: University of Massachusetts Press, 1987.

Jakobson, Roman. *Verbal Art, Verbal Sign, Verbal Time*, edited by Krystyna Pomorska and Stephen Rudy. Minneapolis: University of Minnesota Press, 1985.

Kaiser, Nancy A. "Faust/Faustine in the Nineteenth Century: Man's Myth, Women's Places." In *Our Faust? Roots and Ramifications of a Modern German Myth*, edited by Reinhold Grimm and Jost Hermand. Madison: University of Wisconsin Press, 1987.

Kastendieck, Miles. "A Unique Experience: A Handsome Show." Review of *Four Saints in Three Acts* by Gertrude Stein. *New York Journal American*, 17 April 1952.

Kellner, Bruce, ed. *A Gertrude Stein Companion: Content with the Example*. Westport, CT: Greenwood Press, 1988.

Kennedy, Andrew. *Six Dramatists in Search of a Language*. London: Cambridge University Press, 1975.

Kerman, Joseph. *Opera as Drama*, rev. ed. Berkeley and Los Angeles: University of California Press, 1988.

Kirby, Michael. *A Formalist Theatre*. Philadelphia: University of Pennsylvania Press, 1987.

Kornfeld, Lawrence. "From a Director's Notebook: How the Curtain Did Come: Conflict and Change: The Theatre of Gertrude Stein." *Performing Arts Journal*, Spring 1976: 33–39.

Kristeva, Julia. "Modern Theater Does Not Take (A) Place." *Sub-Stance*, 18/19 (1977): 131–134.

Langer, Susanne. *Feeling and Form: A Theory of Art*. New York: Charles Scribner's Sons, 1953.

Larthomas, Pierre. *Le Langage dramatique: sa nature, ses procédés*, rev. ed. Paris: Presses Universitaires de France, 1980.

Okerlund, A. N. " 'Be Silent Then, for Danger Is in Words': The Intellectual Folly of Dr. Faustus." In *Reinterpretations of Marlowe's Faustus: A Collection of Critical Essays*, edited by Ghanshiam Sharma. Delhi: Doaba House, 1984.

O'Neill, William. *Everyone Was Brave: A History of Feminism in America*. New York: Quadrangle, 1969.

Pavis, Patrice. *Languages of the Stage: Essays in the Semiology of Theatre*. New York: Performing Arts Journal Publications, 1982.

Poggioli, Renato. *The Theory of the Avant-Garde*, translated by Gerald Fitzgerald. Cambridge, MA: Harvard University Press, 1968.

Porter, David. *Emerson and Literary Change*. Cambridge, MA: Harvard University Press, 1978.

Preston, John Hyde. "A Conversation." *The Atlantic Monthly*, August 1935: 187–194.

Relph, Edward. *Rational Landscapes and Humanistic Geography*. London: Croom Helm, 1981.

Ryan, Betsy Alayne. *Gertrude Stein's Theatre of the Absolute*. Ann Arbor, MI: UMI Research Press, 1984.

Schmitz, Neil. *Of Huck and Alice: Humorous Writing in American Literature*. Minneapolis: University of Minnesota Press, 1983.

Seldes, Gilbert. "Delight in the Theatre." *Review of Four Saints in Three Acts*, by Gertrude Stein. *Modern Music*, March–April 1934: 138–141.

Smith, Barbara Herrnstein. *On the Margins of Discourse*. Chicago: University of Chicago Press, 1978.

Smith, Patrick J. *The Tenth Muse: A Historical Study of the Opera Libretto*. New York: Alfred A. Knopf, 1970.

Stein, Gertrude. *The Autobiography of Alice B. Toklas*. 1933. Reprint, New York: Vintage Books, 1961.

———. *Bee Time Vine and Other Pieces*. New Haven, CT: Yale University Press, 1953.

———. *Composition As Explanation*. London: Hogarth Press, 1926. Reprinted in *Look at Me Now and Here I Am: Writings and Lectures 1909–45*, edited by Patricia Meyerowitz. Harmondsworth: Penguin Books, 1971.

———. Correspondence and Manuscript Notebooks, Gertrude Stein Papers, Yale Collection of American Literature, Beinecke Rare Book and Manuscript Library, Yale University.

———. *Everybody's Autobiography*. 1937. Reprint, New York: Vintage Books, 1973.

———. *Fernhurst, Q.E.D., and Other Early Writings*. New York: Liveright, 1971.

———. *The Geographical History of America or the Relation of Human Nature to the Human Mind*. 1935. Reprint, New York: Vintage Books, 1973.

———. *Geography and Plays*. 1922. Reprint, New York: Something Else Press, 1968.

———. *The Gertrude Stein First Reader and Three Plays*. Boston: Houghton Mifflin Company, 1948.

———. *How to Write*. 1931. Reprint, West Glover, VT: Something Else Press, 1973.

———. Interview by William Lundell, 12 October 1934. Typescript. Gertrude Stein Papers, Yale Collection of American Literature, Beinecke Rare Book and Manuscript Library, Yale University.

———. *Last Operas and Plays*. 1949. Reprint, New York: Vintage Books, 1975.

———. *Lectures in America*. 1935. Reprint, Boston: Beacon Press, 1985.

———. *Operas and Plays*. 1932. Reprint, Barrytown, NY: Station Hill Press, 1987.

———. *Painted Lace and Other Pieces*. New Haven, CT: Yale University Press, 1955.

———. *Picasso: The Complete Writings*, edited by Edward Burns. Boston: Beacon Press, 1985.

————. *Portraits and Prayers*. New York: Random House, 1934.

————. *Reflection on the Atomic Bomb: Volume I of the Previously Uncollected Writings of Gertrude Stein*, edited by Robert Bartlett Haas. Los Angeles: Black Sparrow Press, 1973.

————. *Selected Writings*, edited by Carl Van Vechten. New York: Random House, 1946.

————. *Stanzas in Meditation and Other Poems*. New Haven, CT: Yale University Press, 1956.

————. *Useful Knowledge*. New York: Payson and Clarke, 1928.

————. *A Village. Are You Ready Yet Not Yet. A Play in Four Acts*. Paris: Galerie Simon, 1928.

Steiner, Wendy. *Exact Resemblance to Exact Resemblance: The Literary Portraiture of Gertrude Stein*. New Haven, CT: Yale University Press, 1978.

Stewart, Allegra. *Gertrude Stein and the Present*. Cambridge, MA: Harvard University Press, 1967.

Stimpson, Catharine R. "The Mind, the Body, and Gertrude Stein." *Critical Inquiry*, 3 (Spring 1977): 489–506.

Stokes, John. *Resistible Theatres*. London: Paul Elek Books, 1972.

Styan, John L. *Drama, Stage, and Audience*. London: Cambridge University Press, 1975.

Sutherland, Donald. *Gertrude Stein: A Biography of Her Work*. New Haven, CT: Yale University Press, 1951.

Thomson, Virgil. *The Musical Scene*. New York: Alfred A. Knopf, 1945.

————. *Virgil Thomson*. New York: Alfred A. Knopf, 1966.

Tuan, Yi-Fu. "Thought and Landscape: The Eye and the Mind's Eye." In *The Interpretation of Ordinary Landscapes*, edited by D. W. Meinig. New York: Oxford University Press, 1979.

Van Vechten, Carl. Introduction to *Last Operas and Plays*, by Gertrude Stein. New York: Vintage Books, 1975.

Veltruský, Jiří. "Dramatic Text as a Component of Theater." In *The Semiotics of Art: Prague School Contributions*, edited by Ladislav Matejka and Irwin R. Titunik. Cambridge, MA: MIT Press, 1976.

Weinstein, Norman. *Gertrude Stein and the Literature of the Modern Consciousness*. New York: Frederick Ungar, 1970.

Wittig, Susan. "Toward a Semiotic Theory of the Drama." *Educational Theatre Journal*, 26 (December 1974): 441–454.

Young, Stark. "One Moment Alit." Review of *Four Saints in Three Acts*, by Gertrude Stein. *The New Republic*, 7 March 1934: 105.

Index

This book was set in Baskerville and Eras typefaces. Baskerville was designed by John Baskerville at his private press in Birmingham, England, in the eighteenth century. The first typeface to depart from oldstyle typeface design, Baskerville has more variation between thick and thin strokes. In an effort to insure that the thick and thin strokes of his typeface reproduced well on paper, John Baskerville developed the first wove paper, the surface of which was much smoother than the laid paper of the time. The development of wove paper was partly responsible for the introduction of typefaces classified as modern, which have even more contrast between thick and thin strokes.

Eras was designed in 1969 by Studio Hollenstein in Paris for the Wagner Typefoundry. A contemporary script-like version of a sans-serif typeface, the letters of Eras have a monotone stroke and are slightly inclined.

Printed on acid-free paper.